THE SALVAGE OF **THE KURSK**

Alexander Bakker & Lars Walder

This is a SMIT Salvage production
WWW.SMIT.COM

Authors: Alexander Bakker & Lars Walder

Photography: Mammoet / SMIT, Hans de Jong Maritime Pictures, Edwin Otter OW tv, Piet Sinke
Illustrations: ANP, Bumblebee Studios
Lay-out: Studio Clarenburg
Offsetprinting: Schefferdrukkerij B.V.

ISBN: 90-9017034-0

CONTENTS

A WORD OF GRATITUDE

How swiftly is the world changing! Quite recently I as the Head of a large Russian design bureau specialised, mainly, in design of, perhaps, one of the most secret types of military equipment - submarines, could not even imagine that I would be a participant of a large-scale international project. It was not just an international project because we, in CDB ME 'Rubin', got used to international projects, but a project that did not have analogues in the history - the salvage project of a Russian submarine!

Analysing this phenomenon I can find the only explanation of this: technological progress of the mankind that formed necessary conditions for creation of weapons and armament of tremendous destructive abilities forced people to realise, at last, fragility and vulnerability of our world as well as the value of each human life. Possessing a huge destructive potential the mankind has no right to be an indifferent observer of any tragedy irrespective of place where it happened. This new understanding by the Human Being of his predestination and responsibility for the fate of the World ceases to be 'the religion' of a sole person.

Millions of people all over the world perceived the tragedy of Russian submarine 'Kursk' as their own pain. The disaster of submarine 'Kursk' was taken by an international society not only as a tragedy of her crew - 118 men perished in the first minutes and hours of the accident. The ship lying on the sea bed at the depth of a little more than 100 meter was considered also as a source of potential threat to the environment that had to be eliminated as soon as possible. All of us were united: Russians, Dutch, Norwegians, Scots and people of many other countries taking part in the 'Kursk' salvage operation..

I would like to come back to the interdependence between the progress of technology and mankind's evolution.

A swift progress of technique and technology inevitably entails technogenic catastrophes. Eventually, this is the mankind's payment for progress in many fields of our life (possibility of fast travelling practically to any distance, heat and light in our houses etc.). That's why natural cataclysms (destructive earthquakes, tsunami, hurricanes, floods etc.) are taken by the mankind as an inevitable evil, but in case of technogenic disasters we are always looking for the answer to questions: who is guilty and why it could happen.

Modern technique and technology allow creating objects possessing a huge destructive force or objects that can be sources of potential technogenic catastrophes. The same technique and technology allow solving tasks of decreasing the probability of such catastrophes and elimination of their consequences. International operation of the 'Kursk' salvage is just such an example of using technological and intellectual potential of the mankind.

From the technological point of view the 'Kursk' salvage is a fantastic fusion of achievements in various fields. These are technologies of complex diving works, underwater cutting of super strong steel of the submarine hull, lifting of super heavy loads, compensation of dynamic forces arising in the lifting rigs as a result of seaways, computerised control of the lifting system. Application of mentioned technologies was accompanied by unique and bold designer's solutions.

Nevertheless, it was human technology that was the most important in our joint project: our ability to look for operative solution of complicated problems together, to find common language, to agree in difficult situations and ability to work as a Team.

By lifting the 'Kursk' from the bed of the Barents Sea our international team has shown to the entire world an excellent example of co-operation in the name of solving problems common to the mankind. That's why I am proud that I was a part of the grandiose salvage project of submarine 'Kursk' and I would like to express my gratitude to all who did not spare themselves working over the execution of our common brave plan. I am grateful to the Management of Smit who were among the first who responded to the 'Kursk' tragedy and lent a helping hand. I am grateful to the Management of Mammoet who made a brave decision – to become the chief contractor of the project based on a principally new technology. I am grateful to managers and specialists of many Russian and foreign companies who managed within extremely short period of time to do what seemed to be impossible - to prepare and carry out the 'Kursk' salvage operation. I was convinced of high profes-sionalism and responsibility of all participants of works and saw that we could efficiently work together with our foreign partners on the most chal-lenging projects.

I would like to express my special gratitude to the international crews of ships who participated in various stages of the operation (Diving Support Vessel Mayo, barges AMT Carrier and Giant 4, MSV Regalia) as well as to Russian navy men who undertook a difficult task of providing support to the 'Kursk' sal-vage operation, submarine transportation and docking as well as providing safety in the area of the operation.

My feelings are shared by specialists of Central Design Bureau for Marine Engineering Rubin who tried, together with Dutch specialists, to find the most reliable and safe method of the 'Kursk' lifting and who worked onboard the mentioned vessels in international teams. Good luck to you, my friends! I wish you success and wellbeing.

Igor D. Spassky

General Designer – Head of CDB ME Rubin,
Academician of Russian Academy of Sciences

FOREWORD

With a history of more than 160 years, SMIT has a lot of experience with remarkable operations. Especially in salvage we have a track record that is well known worldwide. However the salvage of the Russian submarine 'Kursk' was for SMIT certainly an enormous milestone. Not only because of the complexity of the operation, but also because of the enormous tragedy that involved the loss of so many highly qualified seamen.

For the Russian people, the sinking of their flagship 'Kursk' had an enormous impact. As a Dutch company, specialized in marine services, we are very proud that we were able to help the Russian authorities in bringing the 'Kursk' back home, together with all bodies of the victims.

This book tells the story of the salvage operation. It describes many technical details, inventions, problems and successes.
In operations like this all credits go to those who are in the spotlight. In this case SMIT, together with Mammoet, its partner in this operation, were complemented many times. We were even honored by the Russian President Mr. Putin. However, the operation would never have been a success without the tremendous help of many subcontractors. It is impossible to mention all their work here, but their names are mentioned in this book.

Finally, I wish to thank the Russian design bureau Rubin, and especially Mr. Igor D. Spassky, for his uncompromising effort to make this operation to a success. Also all the work and effort of the staff of SMIT and Mammoet in often very difficult circumstances is something to be very grateful for.

I wish you a lot of reading pleasure with this well documented book.

Ben Vree
Chairman of the Executive Board of SMIT

*Part of the crew before the 'Kursk' left the port. Shortly before they set sail,
they won an award as best submarine crew of the Russian Northern Fleet.*

*The precise location of the sunken 'Kursk':
69° 37'00" North, 37° 34'25" East*

THE SINKING

As the submarine 'Kursk' sails from the port of Vidiayevo at ten o'clock on the morning of Thursday 10 August 2000, its captain - Gennadiy Liachin - is entitled to feel pleased. His crew has just been awarded the title of best submarine crew in the Russian Northern Fleet. The weather is fine and an exercise in the Barents Sea awaits. The 'Kursk' has 118 people on board for this journey; 111 crew members, five officers from the headquarters of the Submarine Division of the Northern Fleet and two specialists on torpedo weapons, one of them a civilian.

In accordance with the exercise plan 'Kursk' is to fire a training torpedo on Saturday 12 August. It is likely that at this time the 'Kursk' is travelling at low speed at periscope depth. According to regulations, after completion of a torpedo launch the submarine has to report to the Commander of the Northern Fleet about completion of an exercise and leaving the firing range. By 10 o'clock that evening no such report is ever received. Not receiving the report The Commander of the Northern Fleet Admiral V. Popov gives an order to start the search & rescue force deployment.

That Saturday morning, sonarmen of the cruiser 'Petr Velikiy' (Peter the Great) and other ships in the area of the exercises recorder two hydrodynamic blows and the second one was stronger than the first. The two large explosions are also recorded at various locations around the world. The first explosion registers 1.1 on the Richter scale, with the second, 134 seconds later, registering 2.8. Experts have calculated that the first explosion must have been equivalent to the explosion of 0.09 to 0.15 metric tonnes

The showpiece of the Russian navy in the bay at Murmansk.

The explosion occurred in the foremost compartment, where the torpedoes were stored. The depth the sub was at prevented the explosion's shockwave from forcing its way out of the sub; instead, most of the force of the blast travelled through the vessel's interior, causing devastation.

of TNT, with the second equivalent to four tonnes of TNT. Both explosions, it is later revealed, occurred in the fore body of the 'Kursk', that is, in its torpedo chamber.

Both explosions, but naturally the second in particular, create a massive shockwave, most of which travels through the vessel itself. The foremost compartment of the 'Kursk' is very badly damaged, leaving nothing much but a pile of twisted steel. It has not yet been established whether the 'Kursk' sunk immediately after

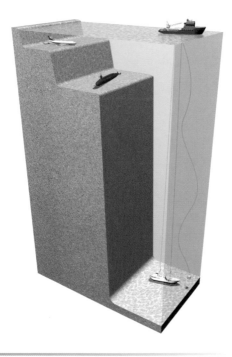

The 'Kursk' lay at a depth of 108 metres. At the same time as the 'Kursk' salvage operation was being carried out, SMIT was raising the Japanese fishing boat 'Ehime Maru' from a depth of 600 metres, which is still the deepest successful salvage operation ever performed. SMIT was also the salvor that raised the TWA Boeing that had crashed off the eastern coast of the United States.

the first explosion or only after the second one. What is clear is that the 'Kursk' was found on the seabed of the Barents Sea at a depth of about 108 metres. Her position: 69° 37′00″ North, 37° 34′25″ East.

'Peter the Great', the flagship of the Russian navy, stays close to the salvage vessels throughout the operation.

It looks like neither the jolt with which the 'Kursk' hit the seabed of the Barents Sea nor the force of the two explosions damaged the two nuclear reactors in compartment six of the submarine and luckily all safety systems would probably have worked perfectly.

At this time, the cause of the 'Kursk' disaster is not officially known but there are plenty of theories. They range from a collision with a Western submarine to a depth charge dropped by the flagship of the Northern Fleet, the cruiser 'Petr Velikiy'. The most probable cause, however, is an accident with an experimental torpedo.

In the early hours of Sunday morning, the cruiser 'Mikhail Rudnitsky' makes sonar contact with an as yet unknown vessel on the floor of the Barents Sea. It just has to be, and is, the 'Kursk'. A few hours later, Russian President Vladimir Putin being outside Moscow, receives a report that the 'Kursk' has been found and that a rescue operation is underway. Multiple efforts of rescue underwater vehicles to mate with the aft rescue

Depiction of the tragedy. The first, minor explosion causes the 'Kursk'
to lose its buoyancy and sink. There is a fire in the torpedo chamber.

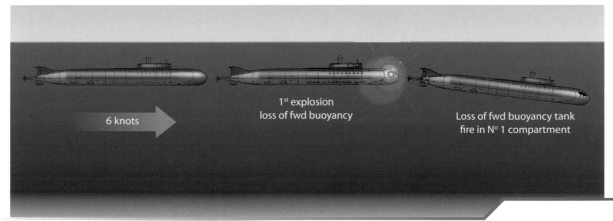

6 knots

1st explosion
loss of fwd buoyancy

Loss of fwd buoyancy tank
fire in N° 1 compartment

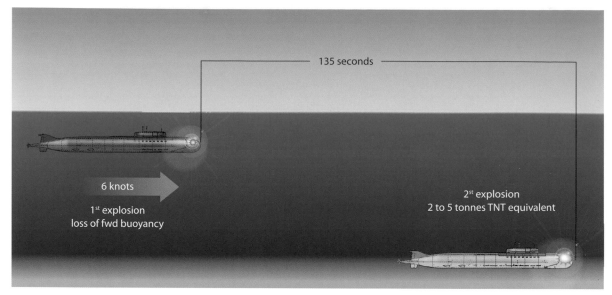

135 seconds

6 knots

1ˢᵗ explosion
loss of fwd buoyancy

2ˢᵗ explosion
2 to 5 tonnes TNT equivalent

A little more than two minutes after the first jolt, the entire torpedo compartment explodes. It's now literally a full-blown disaster.

hatch of the 'Kursk' fail. At 11 o'clock in the morning of Monday 14 August, the spokesman for the Northern Fleet informs the Russian media of 'problems' on board the nuclear submarine 'Kursk'.

On Saturday 12 August at 11.30 in the evening Admiral Popov, the Commander of the Northern Fleet, declares: 'Consider submarine 'Kursk' in emergency. Start the full-scope search and rescue operation of distressed submarine.' Twenty ships and vessels are sent on a new rescue operation but all attempts fail, as they have not been given the right equipment. Later, actions of the Russian Navy's rescue specialists will be heavily criticised as well. On 15 August representatives of the Main Naval Headquarters go to Brussels for negotiating the possibility of assistance to Russia by NATO countries. In compliance with achieved agreements on 17 August a ship carrying a specially adapted British rescue submarine sets sail from a Norwegian port.

The rescue submarine does not arrive at the 'Kursk' until 20 August, but is unable to open the escape hatches. Norwegian divers are more successful, but only after repeated attempts. When the lower cover of the air lock hatch of the 'Kursk' is finally opened the next day, the rescuers discover that the lower section has completely filled up with water. On this day, it is officially reported that the crew of the 'Kursk' have died.

Later, in October, there is an attempt to rescue the bodies of the dead crew from the sunken 'Kursk'. Twelve bodies are recovered. A note is found on the body of Captain-Lieutenant Dmitriy Kolesnikov. 'It seems that there are no chances, 10 - 20 %', he writes. 'Here is the list of men who gathered in compartment 9 and will try to go out. Hello to everybody, don't loose hope.'

The outskirts of Murmansk are the location for an old building that houses the museum for the Russian Northern Fleet. The museum now has its own room dedicated to the 'Kursk'. The walls are bedecked with a large number of photos and photomontages. Between them, they tell the six-year history of the nuclear submarine 'Kursk'. From the cradle to the grave, from launching to sinking.

There are many cheerful photomontages. Of the day the 'Kursk' was put into service. Of the visitors and crew, on board and at home. With wives, girlfriends, with their children. Family snaps too. Wedding photos, holidays. Open days on board. Children peering through the periscope. With their fathers on top of the conning tower. All cheerful people.

However, the final montages are anything but cheerful. They are pictures of the desperation of the surviving relatives, gathered together and united in grief. Sobbing girlfriends, wives, mothers and other family members. Photos of memorial services; people weeping as they place their wreaths and flowers. Photos too of the boat trip to the place where the 'Kursk' sunk on 12 August 2000. Bottles are filled with seawater drawn by bucket from the exact spot in the Barents Sea where the submarine sank.

There are also photos of the ceremony during which Admiral Vyacheslav Popov, the commander of the Northern Fleet, presents posthumous heroes' medals for the crew members to the surviving relatives. And of course there are photos from the major memorial service held in the naval town of Severomorsk on 29 October 2000. That day it snowed, and the photos show people, adults and children alike, weeping and taking refuge behind the snow-covered guard of honour that is saluting their heroes.

Hidden amongst all these photos is one that says it all. A naval harbour, the 'Kursk' home base. In the distance, a snow-covered moored submarine. In the foreground, with her back to the photographer, a young woman, the profile of her face visible. She presses a child to herself. Both are huddled into the turned-up collar of her coat. The woman looks heartbroken. She knows that the 'Kursk' will never return.

The drama of the 'Kursk' does not just make a deep impression on Russians. The nightmare of being confined to a submarine trapped far below the surface of the sea is one that many can imagine. During those couple of days when there was still hope that there would be some survivors, the whole world followed the rescue operation. When it became clear that there were no survivors, messages of condolence poured in to the Kremlin from all over the world.

In the spring of 2001, two Dutch companies start work on the salvage the 'Kursk'. They are Mammoet, a company specialising in lifting work, and SMIT, the towage and salvage company. Although onlookers are kept away from the actual salvage location, the whole world is watching the operation. It's a race against the clock, where the changeable weather conditions in the Barents Sea are the salvors' greatest enemy.

The salvors always feel the burden of responsibility. On the one hand, the Russian President Putin personally has taken the decision about the submarine lifting and promised the surviving relatives of the

118 passengers and crew who died that the 'Kursk' will be raised before the end of 2001. On the other, the time for successful preparation is very short and the salvors cannot and will not permit themselves to fail. The salvage contract was not signed until May 2001, which gives the salvors just five months to successfully complete this extremely complex operation. This is because the Barents Sea's stormy season starts in October. This is Mammoet's first

SMIT has a (very good) reputation in the field of salvage operations. The company has assisted in all major disasters and salvage operations during the last forty years, including the 'Herald of Free Enterprise' ferry that was raised after capsizing in 1985.

lifting assignment at sea, while SMIT in turn has a (very good) reputation to maintain. Also the client, Russian designers bureau Rubin in St. Peterburg, takes an enormous responsibility to its shoulders.

THE CONTRACT

The report about the loss of the nuclear submarine 'Kursk' does not remain a secret for long. At SMIT in Rotterdam, Geert Koffeman hears the news on Monday 14 August, two days after the loss of the vessel. He immediately contacts Rubin, the Russian navy's design bureau in St. Petersburg. Rubin's director, Igor Spassky, is still very much aware of SMIT's name. In 1989, SMIT was involved in plans to salvage another sunken nuclear submarine, the 'Komsomolets'. This submarine lay at the great depth of 1700 metres and was to be salvaged with participation of SMIT. At that time too, Spassky was head of the Rubin design bureau. However, the change of the political situation in the world and in Russia(the fall of the Berlin Wall) that same year put paid to the salvaging of the 'Komsomolets'.

Cross-section of the 'Kursk'. The foremost compartment has been completely destroyed by the force of the blast. The shockwave penetrated a long way into the vessel but luckily not as far as the - nuclear - engines.

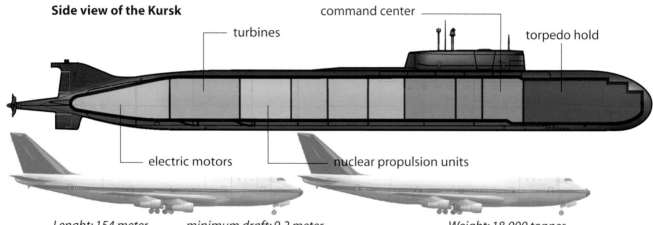

Side view of the Kursk

command center

turbines

torpedo hold

electric motors

nuclear propulsion units

Lenght: 154 meter   *minimum draft: 9.2 meter*   *Weight: 18,000 tonnes*

Width: 18.2 meter   *Displacement: 24,000 tonnes (under water)*   *Power: 190 megawatt/reactor*

In this initial contact with Igor Spassky, Geert Koffeman expresses his condolences and offers SMIT's services. However, there is not much that SMIT can do. Very specialised equipment is needed to open the hatches on the 'Kursk'- equipment that SMIT does not have. However, what SMIT can and does do is to start gathering information on the 'Kursk'. In addition, SMIT's engineers, some of whom have expertise in submarine construction, are drummed up. The arrangements made between SMIT and the Dutch Royal Navy's submarine unit regarding assistance in the event of a Dutch submarine disaster prove useful, as does the wealth of experience gained by SMIT president Nico Buis, who used to be both a vice-admiral and a submarine commander.

In Rotterdam, SMIT receives information from many sources, including former crew members of Russian subs. There are even so-called experts who are able to entice the Rotterdam salvors to London with their talk of a revolutionary method for raising the 'Kursk'. In the bathroom of a London hotel, a bathtub demonstration is given of how the hapless sub can be frozen and so rise to the surface like a block of ice! In Brussels in the early autumn of 2000, the Kursk Foundation is set up, headed by the former Dutch

Defence Minister Wim van Eekelen and the former Russian Foreign Minister Alexander Bessmertnykh. The man behind the Foundation is the Brussels lobbyist Rio Praaning, joint owner of the lobbying and PR agency Praaning Meines. The Foundation is concerned about possible environmental consequences of the disaster in the Barents Sea caused by the nuclear reactors on board the 'Kursk' and works hard to obtain both international cooperation in this matter and the necessary funds. The Kursk Foundation succeeds in getting the Dutch government to provide about EUR 225,000 to the Russian authorities for research into possible options for the salvage of the 'Kursk'.

Initially, the Kursk Foundation is able to gain the support of the Russian vice-premier Ilya Klebanov, who is made responsible for the operation to salvage the 'Kursk', by promising to raise half the estimated total sum of seventy million EUR required. An attempt is made to organise the salvage of the 'Kursk' under an EU environmental programme.

At a press conference in Brussels, the Kursk Foundation expresses its support for Mammoet-SMIT's salvage plans.

l. to r.: Nico Buis (SMIT) Frans van Seumeren (Mammoet), Wim van Eekelen and Alexander Bessmertnikh (both of the Kursk Foundation).

The world's press closely monitors all developments regarding the 'Kursk'.

At SMIT in Rotterdam, it soon becomes apparent that the best approach would be to undertake the 'Kursk' salvage operation using 'proven technology'. After all, the operation is not exactly without risk. And it is clear that a consortium will have to be formed, with such long-standing partners as the Leiden offshore group Heerema and the American company Halliburton. SMIT wants to 'just hoist up' the 'Kursk'. This approach would require the deployment of Heerema's semi-submersible crane vessel 'Thialf', although the problem here is that the 'Thialf' cannot and is not permitted to sail with a load in its rigging. In order to overcome this problem, the lifting cables will have to be fed straight down through a large barge. Under this method, the 'Kursk' is to be hoisted and pulled against the underside of the barge and held there.

The plan is quickly approved by Rubin, the Russian navy's design bureau, which, during the autumn of 2000 has been the recipient of many salvage plans. In December, SMIT, Heerema and Halliburton start the negotiations regarding the salvage assignment. It is clear that a decision will have to be made by the end of January if the 'Kursk' is to be raised before the winter of 2001. After all, this is what President Putin has now promised the surviving relatives of the crew. The aim is to carry out the salvage operation in August.

Depiction of the lifting plan. A barge equipped with 26 lifting units is to raise the 'Kursk' horizontally to the surface. The lifting cables are attached to the frames using large grippers (plugs). This requires the cutting of holes in the sub's exterior and interior shells.

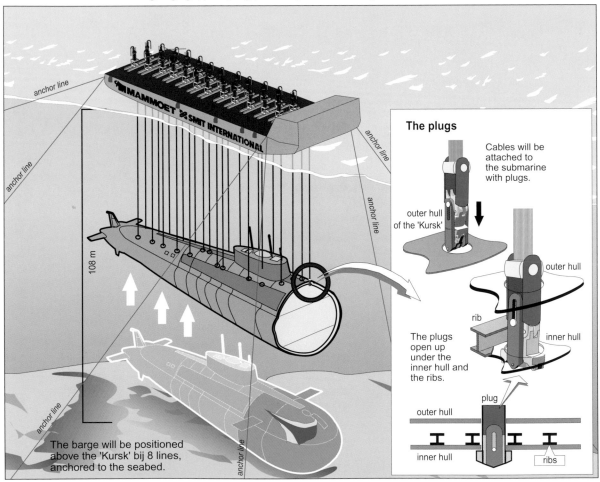

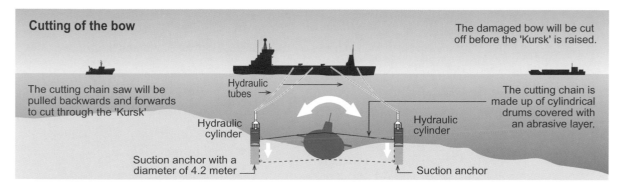

Cutting of the bow

The damaged bow will be cut off before the 'Kursk' is raised.

The cutting chain saw will be pulled backwards and forwards to cut through the 'Kursk'

The cutting chain is made up of cylindrical drums covered with an abrasive layer.

Hydraulic tubes →

Hydraulic cylinder

Hydraulic cylinder

Suction anchor with a diameter of 4.2 meter

Suction anchor

Before lifting can commence, the badly damaged bow has to be cut off. SMIT designs a special cutting wire for this job that is to be placed over the nose and 'saw' its way through it and down to the seabed.

The negotiations between the Russian government and the Dutch-American consortium focus on the profound study of the 'Kursk' lifting method as well as on financial guarantees and the payment schedule, as the Russians now have the funding they need. This is because the Russian government has agreed to pay for the salvage operation itself as it is not sure that the Kursk Foundation will be able to raise the required funds. However, the operation still needs to get underway soon, not only because it will require about thirteen thousand hours of engineering work but also because Heerema needs the 'Thialf' for another job in late autumn.

In mid-April, and in secrecy, Frans van Seumeren and Mammoet's Russian director Slava Zacharov are summoned to St. Petersburg. Rubin feels that the negotiations with the consortium that SMIT belongs to are getting bogged down. The main stumbling block is that it appears that the consortium can no longer carry out the salvage operation during 2001, simply because the necessary equipment cannot be made available in time.

The two directors of the joint venture: Nico Buis (SMIT) and Frans van Seumeren (Mammoet).

Other sticking points are the payment guarantees and the question of which country's legislation is to be applied to the contract. During the secret meeting, Rubin boss Spassky asks the crucial question: can Mammoet still salvage the 'Kursk' this year? If it can, it will get the contract. Returning to De Meern, Van Seumeren discusses options with his engineers. A few days later, he informs Spassky that as far as Mammoet is concerned, the salvage operation can still be carried out in 2001.

It is now the end of April and deadlines continue to slide. In the early morning of 16 May, Rubin's boss Igor Spassky informs SMIT's consortium that it has lost the contract because it can no longer carry out the salvage operation in 2001. It is thanked for all of its efforts.

At this time, a Mammoet delegation has already been in St. Petersburg as Rubin's guests for several days. The plans are drawn up during the night and recalculated and accordingly are ready in a Russian version the next morning.

Van Seumeren asks Spassky to sign the declaration of intent drawn up in the Netherlands and faxed to him. At that time, those involved at Mammoet are convinced that the deal can be signed. However, Van Seumeren and his associates also know that Rubin is taking a big gamble by going for Mammoet, as the latter has no experience in the field of salvaging. This viewpoint is later echoed by vice-premier Ilya Klebanov: 'Mammoet was not one of those chosen for the original tender but we could not delay the whole operation by a year. Using Mammoet meant that, in theory, it could all still be done in 2001. We took this chance, but it was a risk.'

The Russians accept the proposal to deposit the entire salvage fee in a Dutch bank account. In addition, a down payment of 16 million dollars is made. The entire salvage operation is then divided into stages. Payment for a particular stage is to follow after a specific type of deed for that stage has been drafted and signed by both parties.

SMIT is now asking itself exactly who has actually won the contract. The answer is not long in coming, as the salvage world is buzzing with stories that lifting specialist Mammoet of De Meern, The Netherlands, has ordered components for so-called strandjacks (lifting jacks). SMIT chief executive Nico Buis doesn't hesitate for a second - he calls Frans van Seumeren. 'Congratulations, but you can't do it alone', is the message from Rotterdam.

The next day, Van Seumeren phones Buis to find out whether SMIT would be interested in participating in the 'Kursk' salvage operation. The very next day, Buis and Executive Board Member Ben Vree visit the Mammoet headquarters in De Meern. They are in for a long day, as engineers from both companies are summoned in turn to the meeting room. By the evening, an agreement has been drafted for a 50:50 joint venture between Mammoet and SMIT to salvage the 'Kursk'. SMIT is to be responsible for the nautical part of the operation, with Mammoet being responsible for the lifting. That night both teams celebrate their joint venture in a local bar.

It was a high-risk gamble for Rubin boss Spassky, Mammoet and SMIT agree afterwards, as the pressure from Putin and his associates must have been enormous. Nico Buis praises the approach taken by Frans van Seumeren, calls him 'a good bloke', suspects that the Russians must have loved Frans's relaxed approach and also lets Mammoet's Russian director Slava Zacharov take a little of the credit.

Bad weather on the Barents Sea. The salvage team has to complete the job before the storm season begins in October.

In The Netherlands, people are amazed that Van Seumeren was able to win an assignment the whole salvage world wanted. After all, it is very much a maritime-related job, a field in which Mammoet has little experience. Mammoet is even portrayed as 'a second division team'...

THE PREPARATORY STAGE

The barge to be used for the salvage operation is the 'Giant 4'. This semi-submersible SMIT barge is normally used for on-deck loading, but this time the load will be suspended under the barge itself.

The salvor's plan involves using a large single barge, on which the strandjacks complete with sea swell compensation units must be fitted. Lifting cables have to be fed straight down through the barge and part of the underside of the barge itself will have to be cut away to make room for the 'Kursk's conning towers.

Another problem is the foremost compartment of the 'Kursk', which is badly damaged. After all, this was where the torpedoes, which have all exploded, were located. This means, as the Russian authorities insist during the negotiations, that the sub's 'nose' will have to be sawn off. Later, the salvor's themselves see the damaged section as a risk, as anything could happen if this part of the 'Kursk' were to break off during the lifting operation.

Even when the 'Kursk' operation is well underway, the salvor's still have many problems to overcome. The preparation period is extremely short. All leave is cancelled, although no order actually needs to be given for this. In fact, it is amazing what incredible sacrifices the employees of both companies are prepared to make to assist the salvage operation.

Rubin monitors all of the preparations closely. Apart from the operational work, the salvage team is given a mountain of official paperwork to complete. All technical details and specifications must be recorded in writing. Understandably, the Russian authorities have innumerable questions that need answering, amounting to four or five A4 sheets' worth a day. In many cases, the questions relate to matters that the salvage team has not even considered yet. Rubin employs 1,800 highly trained engineers, one hundred of whom are released to work on the 'Kursk' project. As a result, both Mammoet's and SMIT's engineers, who are far fewer in number, have their hands full. Rubin wants to see rock-solid theory underpinning all practical aspects of the operation, whereas the salvors are used to playing many things 'by ear'. Throughout the operation, the collaboration between the Russians and Dutch steadily improves, as does their mutual respect.

In respect of the technology to be deployed, only the strandjacks are familiar territory. The swell compensation system is being used on such a large scale for the first time, and the plugs or 'grippers' that will have to attach the lifting cables to the 'Kursk' still have to be designed, developed, manufactured and tested.

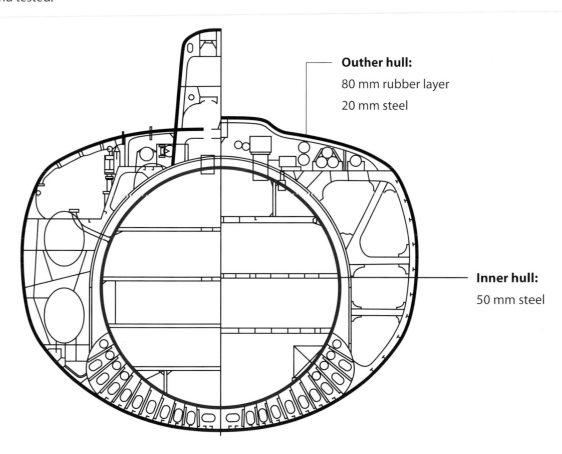

Outher hull:
80 mm rubber layer
20 mm steel

Inner hull:
50 mm steel

Cross-section of the 'Kursk'. Divers have to cut 26 holes through the exterior shell and the (red) interior shell. The holes will also have to be cleared of all cables and pipelines that lie between the two shells. The exterior shell is covered with a layer of thick rubber to minimise sonar reflection.

Later on, another problem surfaces regarding the lifting cables: where do you store 26 bundles each of 54 cables that are each 150 metres long? The original plan is to simply store the bundles on deck, but the preferred option, it soon appears, is to coil these cables on spools. To prevent the cables jamming, a special spool is developed that can coil each of the 54 cables separately.

Special developed plugs for this salvage operation. They can secure theirselves under the inner hull and the ribs of the 'Kursk'.

The basic idea for the use of grippers (plugs) comes from the Rubin engineers. They are also able to indicate points on the 'Kursk' that are strong enough for the grippers to be attached to. However, they do not make things easy for the Dutch salvors. The holes to be made in the hull of the 'Kursk' cannot exceed 700 millimetres in diameter and the grippers themselves must not protrude more than 75 centimetres into the submarine. Very tough requirements are also set regarding the grippers' strength.

The salvors are in luck, as it is summer, a time when few companies are really busy. Dozens of subcontractors are contracted to manufacture the grippers and the spools for the cable, and for the thousand and one other things needed. All companies co-operate extremely well.

Huisman-Itrec in Schiedam (NL) designs and manufactures the huge grippers, which is an incredible feat in itself. The first two are used at the end of July for extensive tests, the most important of these being carried out at the Krylov Institute in St. Petersburg. As if from nothing, a re-created part of the sub's hull has appeared. A tension-testing machine is used to test the strength of the grippers. At a force of 2,100 tonnes, the machine starts creaking and groaning, but the test gripper doesn't flinch.
The Russians approve the follow-up production, but have cause to give a strange look when informed that the rest of the grippers are as good as ready. The salvage team had to continue its work, and pressure of time made it imperative to start the manufacturing process for the remaining 24 grippers immediately.

SMIT has plenty of experience in sawing-through ships' hulls, but what is even more important is that for some time now the company has been working in-house on ways of improving its sawing techniques. For a couple of years now, SMIT's Research and Development Department (R&D), has been working with the engineering department to find ways of further improving their most common technique, which is

The cutting wire is tested on an old sand dredger near Rotterdam. As expected, the wire proves highly suitable for cutting through the thick steel.

to saw with a heavy chain and brute force. The engineers know that there is little point in using a diamond saw on steel, as the great frictional heat generated would reduce the diamond to carbon.

Recently a new system has been devised, under which a chain or cable is to be wrapped in sleeves made from joined pieces of ultra-hard steel. By sheer coincidence, this new saw was tested for the first time just two weeks before the sinking of the 'Kursk'. One month later, a second test was carried out at a breaker's yard in 's-Gravendeel (NL).

The wire consists of a chain wrapped in sleeves covered in pieces of 'widia', a diamond-like material.

◀ *In the Norwegian port of Kirkenes, a piece of steel like the steel used in the Kursk's hull is being sawn through. Towards the rear of the deck, part of one of the suction anchors (which house the saw's driving mechanism) can be seen.*

After the test, a team ▶ of experts examines the cutting wire. It is still in development, which means continual modifications are made.

At the time that SMIT's salvage teams and the engineers are asked to help with the sawing-off of the 'Kursk's' nose, the saw is not yet ready for this task. People put their heads together to decide on the correct design and technique. The decision is taken to go for large suction anchors on opposite sides of the 'Kursk' to guide the sawing cable. The drive is to be provided by winches fitted on board two tugs. Even when this decision is taken, there are still doubts. Theo Haak, R&D manager: 'We felt that it wouldn't work.' Accordingly, all engineers are brought together once again to work on a new plan, which is completed just one day later. The tugs are replaced by hydraulic cylinders that are to be fitted

on top of the suction anchors. However, this creates a major problem: where will SMIT get all of the necessary components in such a short time?

'Luckily, we were able to get many things delivered', recalls Theo Haak. 'All our suppliers wanted to help. Components that would normally take 8 months to deliver were ready in just a couple of weeks.'

The hydraulic cylinders required were taken from three old wrecking cranes and converted into two 'new' ones for underwater operation (new cylinders

◀ *In order to prevent overheating, the saw and the steel are cooled with water.*

have a delivery period of twenty weeks). The cylinders, five metres long and 50 centimetres in diameter, are fitted to huge suction anchors. To provide the power, Mammoet uncovered some old powerpacks from a previous job in Alaska. Haak: 'Their capacity was actually a little bit too low, but it would have cost a lot more to lease new units.'

The joint venture with SMIT also involves the deployment of the barge 'Giant 4'. This semi-submersible 140-metre long and 36-metre wide barge is normally used for loading material onto its deck. For this job, however, the load is to be held under the barge. This means that the 'Giant 4' will have to be extensively rebuilt. But where can this be done at such short notice? At the very last moment, a site is found at the Shipdock shipyard in Amsterdam, which gives the salvors every assistance. In a very short time, the 'Giant 4' is transformed. For weeks on end, hundreds of people work extremely hard on the conversion, from very early in the morning to very late at night. In doing so, many see their holidays go by the board.

On the engineers' instructions, large pieces of steel are cut away from the floor to make room for the Kursk' conning towers. This hole is cut to a size of 30.6 by 8.44 metres. To compensate for this, the structure is strengthened at various points with about 2,000 tonnes of steel. In addition, so-called saddles are

The 'Giant 4' barge arrives at Shipdock in Amsterdam, where it will have
to be extensively rebuilt before it can begin its voyage to the Barents Sea.

The deck of the 'Giant 4' (floor area 4,320 m²) still looks bare. This is where the 26 lifting units will be placed, along with accommodation for about 50 salvage workers.

fixed to the floor of the 'Giant-4', against which the 'Kursk' will be held once it has been hoisted up.

Furthermore, 26 conduits are drilled straight down through the barge, through which the lifting cables will be fed. On top of these the lifting units are placed: each a platform holding the five-metre high cylinders of the swell compensation system and the strandjacks, and on top of the latter the cable spools. A complete assembly line to put all the units together is constructed alongside the 'Giant 4' on the quay. After just the first few weeks, the salvors have made excellent progress.

One of the holes to which a lifting unit will be fitted. The hole measures 1,000 mm.

The underside of the 'Giant 4'. The first pipe through which the lifting

cables are to be passed can be fed through from deck to ship bottom.

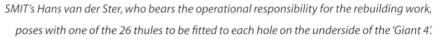

SMIT's Hans van der Ster, who bears the operational responsibility for the rebuilding work,

poses with one of the 26 thules to be fitted to each hole on the underside of the 'Giant 4'.

Saddles fitted to the underside of the 'Giant 4' have the same rounding as the 'Kursk'. These saddles ensure that the sub will remain firmly anchored to the barge for the voyage from the Barents Sea to Murmansk. (See also pages 98-99.)

During the salvage operation itself, about 50 people will be at work on board the 'Giant 4'. The problem is that the vessel has no accommodation itself. It has no propulsion mechanism of its own and always has to be towed, which is why there are no sleeping quarters. Accordingly, the deck of the 'Giant 4' is filled with containers containing berths, a 'canteen' and a galley. Huge tanks containing drinking water are also fitted on deck. The crew will have to 'camp' on the barge for several weeks. Other containers placed on deck contain liquid nitrogen for the swell compensation system as well as all kinds of auxiliary equipment.

At the end of July, Rubin boss Spassky and Admiral Barskov drop in to the Amsterdam site to see how things are going. They are impressed, and it seems that only now do they start believing that the operation could be successful.

However, there is still a great deal of work to be done, in addition to the construction and amassing of all the required equipment and the installation work on the 'Giant 4'. Every piece of equipment has to be described in detail, complete with construction and calculation reports and mode of operation. This is not just a requirement set by Rubin, but is also down to the fact that everything has to be described in really minute detail for insurance and classification purposes.

The lifting jacks, the so-called strandjacks, may be familiar territory for the hoisting specialists, but this is the first time that 26 of these units will be used at the same time. Mammoet always uses the jacks for one-off jobs, such as when it was asked to place the Millennium Wheel, the giant Ferris wheel in the centre of London, in position.

The only problem with the decision to deploy strandjacks is their availability. Mammoet itself has a big stockpile of them but much of the equipment is currently being used for other jobs at an even greater number of locations. Only a small number can be made available. In the end, three-quarters of the 26 jacks required are manufactured especially for this job. Hysdrospex in Hengelo (NL) delivers all specialised hydraulic equipment.

However, not even this task turns out to be plain sailing. This time the summer period proves to be a disadvantage, as many suppliers want to shut their doors. The salvors have to go to a lot of trouble to get all of the equipment

One of the pipes that lead from the deck to the bottom of the 'Giant 4'.

As the weeks go by, more and more pipes appear on the deck of the gigantic barge.

A large hole is bored in the underside of the 'Giant 4' to completely accommodate the conning tower of the 'Kursk'. The hole measures 32 x 9 metres.

A peep into the hole prepared for the conning tower. Here and there, new pieces of steel have been welded onto the hull, to ensure that the barge's rigidity is not affected too much.

they need manufactured in time. In many cases, people sacrifice their holidays, as the salvage team wants to leave port with the 'Giant 4' at the end of August. Normally, most of the equipment would have required a 12-16-week delivery period but in the end everything is delivered in half this time.

The computer system can be used to control twenty strandjacks that are good for a total capacity of 18,000 tonnes. Rubin insists that the salvors have 26 lifting units, based on the fact that the submarine hull damaged by explosions may not withstand the pulling force of a strandjack. Luckily, a computer supplier is able to supply a second control unit, together with software that allows the two computers to work together via a separate server.

The utilisation of sea swell compensation techniques may not be a unique undertaking in the field of hoisting, but its deployment for the salvage of the 'Kursk' certainly is, in particular regarding the amount of equipment used. A single unit consists of four cylinders, each five metres in length. The cylinders are filled with nitrogen, which allows them to be pushed out or pulled in. In this connection, seven tanks filled with liquid nitrogen are loaded on board the 'Giant 4'. In addition, an operating system and control system have to be developed 'just like that'. In the end, the computer system is improved so much by the German whizzkid developers from the IGH company that it can even be used to simulate all kinds of conditions and events. This simulation feature later proves to be a very important success factor.

Along with everybody else involved in the project, SMIT's R&D manager Theo Haak (left) is finding life hectic at the moment. It may be high summer but few employees are taking a holiday.

A problem of a very different nature and complexity is the presence of the two nuclear reactors on board the 'Kursk'. Readings taken in the immediate vicinity of the wreck of the 'Kursk' show that radiation levels have not increased. For the time being, the experts are assuming that all safety systems on board the submarine have worked properly and that both reactors were automatically shut down.

However, this 'knowledge' is not enough to ensure a safe salvage. What could, and will actually, happen to the reactors if the 'Kursk' slips from its cables when being lifted? How safe are the divers? What are the other nuclear risks? As a response to these concerns Rubin issues 'The Operation Safety Certificate' that convinces the salvors of a minimum risk at all stages of the operation.

SMIT does have some experience with such issues, but despite this the company consults a host of experts. As a former director of Greenpeace, SMIT Salvage director Hans van Rooij has the best contacts, and the Kursk Foundation commissions extensive research too. Van Rooij puts the salvors in contact with the offices of the British specialist John Large, a respected authority on these issues. He puts together a research team (Nuclear Co-ordination Group, NCG) that includes British navy specialists. After some understandable grumbling on the part of the Russians, Large and his team are given every assistance.

They are able to map out all of the nuclear-related issues and assess them in the light of Western European safety standards. According to all those involved, this job was a huge challenge, as never before had a fully armed, sunken, heavily damaged nuclear-powered submarine been salvaged.

Each lifting unit consists of 54 cables.

In the end, all experts agree that the risks are minimal but that the salvors will have to be careful. Radiation levels will be constantly monitored during the operation. To this end, Belgian experts from Antwerp Safety Center are brought in who advise and train the salvors to recognise and deal with the potential risks. The Belgian specialists will not only constantly monitor the team members themselves for radiation but will also monitor the area around the 'Kursk'. Dozens of sensors are hung in place during the salvage operation on the Barents Sea. A specialist from the Krylov Institute works onboard the barge together with the experts from Antwerp Safety Center. His sensitive sensors also are installed on the 'Kursk' hull.

Throughout the entire operation, the salvors are subjected to stringent medical checks. The nuclear safety plan consists of four critical protective barriers, namely shells of heat emitting elements, pressure tight 1st contour, equipment space off the reactor compartment, the submarine pressure hull and bulkheads of the 'Kursk' reactor compartment. Should any two of these four elements prove problematical,

Even though it is already 'full speed ahead' on the rebuilding work, engineers are still working on the final calculations and details.

In just six weeks, the deck of the 'Giant 4' has been completely filled with lifting units, heave compensators, nitrogen containers and containers that are serving as the crew's living quarters.

then the lifting operation will have to be halted.

The salvors also contact Greenpeace and the Norwegian environmental organisation Bellona. The Norwegians in particular are very concerned about the 'Kursk', as they are worried that any problem with the reactors could pose a threat to their fishing grounds. Both environmental groups are informed about the salvage operation, including all nuclear-related issues. They are pleased that they have been informed and feel that their curiosity regarding all aspects of the 'Kursk' disaster has been justified.

The nuclear component also makes it difficult to obtain insurance cover for the entire operation. A research report by nuclear arms experts that has been commissioned by the salvors proves a great help to insurance brokers Aon Hudig, but it still takes some doing to insure the 'nuclear' part of the operation. The consortium of Western insurers approached decides the risk is too great, so in the end

The international press is permitted a final walk round the 'Giant 4' shortly before it leaves Amsterdam for the Barents Sea. Project leader Malcolm Dailey explains what's what.

The 'Giant 4' seen from a lifting crane.

it is a consortium of Russian insurers for nuclear-related policies that provides the necessary cover.

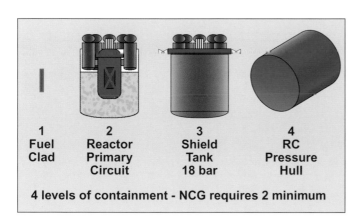

1	2	3	4
Fuel Clad	Reactor Primary Circuit	Shield Tank 18 bar	RC Pressure Hull

4 levels of containment - NCG requires 2 minimum

The onboard reactor has four 'layers' of protection. If two or more of these had been out of order, the salvage team would have advocated the cancellation of the operation. However, an investigation by independent experts has shown that all four protective layers are assumed to be intact.

The gigantic heave compensators have to act as a sort of shock absorber to cancel out the two-to-three metre vertical movement of the barge on the open sea.

The 'Giant 4' leaves the port of Amsterdam for its two-week voyage to the Barents Sea.

Giant spools have been fitted on deck that have to keep several hundred kilometres of cable in place.

The 13-metre high suction anchors were suspended overboard before the voyage taking the sawing materials to the Barents Sea started. This is because it is safer and easier to do this in the sheltered bay at Kirkenes than on the open sea.

At the same time as the 'Giant 4' is leaving Amsterdam, the cutting wire is tested once again in the Norwegian port of Kirkenes. The driving mechanism has been mounted on top of the two huge suction anchors. The anchors will have to be lowered until they are completely 'buried' in the Barents Sea seabed. This will be achieved through suction, which creates a vacuum in these hollow anchors.

THE SALVAGE OPERATION

Throughout the operation, the Scottish company DSND's diving support ship 'Mayo'
serves as the command centre for all the underwater work throughout the operation.

On 6 July, DSND, which was hired for the diving activities, sends the Norwegian diving ship 'Mayo' from Aberdeen to the Barents Sea. The Scottish divers are to be assisted by Russian navy divers, who have specific know-how about Russian weapons, and SMIT's own divers. En route, the divers practise cutting the 26 holes in the 'Kursk's hull with their equipment. They are also informed about the nuclear hazards they may have to face. Jacob Hogendorp is on board for SMIT as coordinator, as SMIT is to carry out the underwater work.

At the YVC shipyard in Bolnes (NL), the saw unit , or at least those parts that are available, is loaded onto the barge 'AMT Carrier'. Many components are still on order and are to be delivered to the Norwegian port of Kirkenes, where the saw unit will actually be constructed. On 19 July, the tug 'Havila Charmer' leaves Rotterdam on its 9-day journey to tow the barge to Kirkenes.

A couple of days before the saw is due to leave Rotterdam, the first team of divers descends to the wreck of the 'Kursk' on the floor of the Barents Sea. Their first job is to flush away the mud using a special 'jetprop' and to clear away all of the pieces of wreckage and other junk. They also start cutting the first of the 26 holes in the hull of the 'Kursk'.

The divers work in three teams, each shift lasting six hours. In order to avoid time-consuming decompression after each dive, the divers deploy the so-called 'saturation technique', under which they breathe a mixture of oxygen and helium. This technique allows them to remain under the same pressure in the pressure tank on board the 'Mayo' for no less than 28 days.

The diving activities are carried out around the clock, 24 hours a day. The divers work in three teams, each shift lasting six hours. In order to avoid the time-consuming process of decompression after every dive, the salvage team uses the so-called saturation technique, whereby the diving teams breathe a mixture

The first images of the 'Kursk', taken by one of the underwater robots known as ROVs (Remotely Operated Vehicles).

A lot of careful manoeuvring is needed in the pressure tank, where the divers sleep, eat and get some rest.

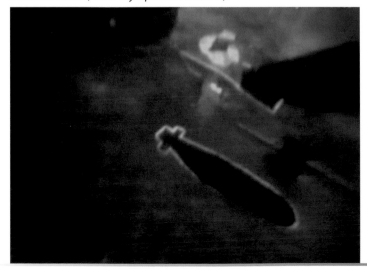

On board the 'Mayo', the divers are closely monitored throughout their work. The divers receive all their instructions from the 'Mayo'.

Divers at work in one of the holes. Armed with portable grinding machines and burners, the areas between the interior and exterior shells are cleared of wiring, pipes and other materials. This will make it easy to lower the grippers (plugs) and position them in the holes later on.

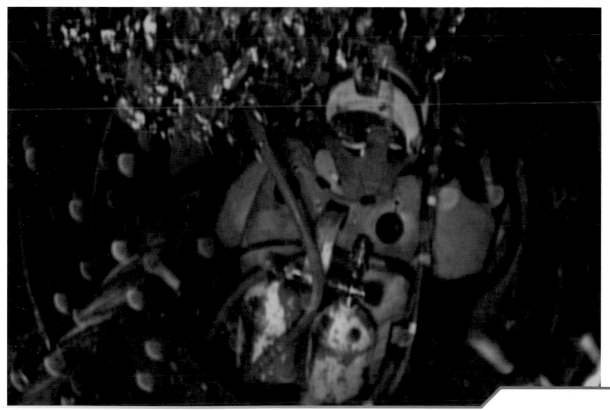

The conning tower of the 'Kursk', showing the sub's logo.

of oxygen and helium. This allows the divers to remain as much as 28 days under the same pressurised conditions, followed by a 4-day decompression period.

The divers descend from the 'Mayo' to the wreck of the 'Kursk' in a diving bell. Two divers carry out the work, with the third remaining behind in the diving bell as their 'protector'. All divers are equipped with helmet-mounted cameras to allow close monitoring of their work from the 'Mayo'. In addition, the diving control room can communicate with the three divers directly. After six hours, the trio are brought up again. Once on board the 'Mayo', the diving bell is connected up to the pressurised living quarters and the next team enters the diving bell.

Diver Peter Smits is checked for possible radiation from the 'Kursk'. A great many of these types of checks will be carried out throughout the entire operation.

There are problems initially with the drilling of the first two holes. The main problem is the rubber cladding of the hull, which was intended to reduce sonar noise. In the end, the divers succeed in removing this cladding with thermal lances. The 26 holes are actually cut by spraying the sub hull with a high-pressure

The divers cut holes in the hull using the 'abrasive jet cutting method'.

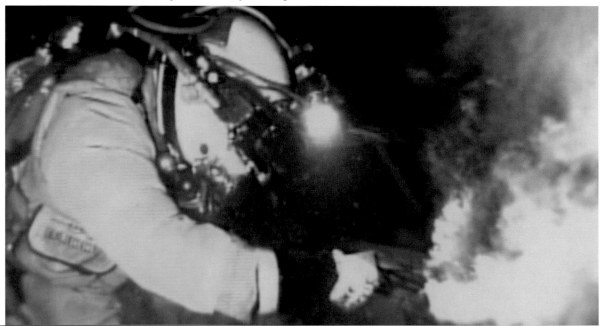

mixture of water and stone dust. This technique proves very suitable for cutting through the steel. Despite the language problems, the divers are greatly helped by the presence of their Russian counterparts. In the final phase of the cutting operation, four SMIT divers are deployed too. SMIT divers do not normally dive at this great depth, which is why they have been given training in saturation diving in Scotland.

The components for the saw start arriving in Kirkenes from all over Europe. At this time, 35 engineers are being accommodated on board the barge 'AMT Carrier' in container quarters. In just a single week, the entire unit has been constructed and computer operating programmes have been written or modified. The first 'dry' test reveals many things, including that the unit works but that the sleeves on the sawing cable are not up to scratch. All fifteen hundred saw sleeves are sent back to Rotterdam for modification. Time is pressing, but a second test carried out a week later is more successful.

The two huge suction anchors have already been suspended under the 'AMT Carrier' before it is towed to the Barents Sea on 20 August, as this work can be done much more safely in the protected bay of Kirkenes than on the open sea. Each anchor is itself more than twelve metres high and has a diameter of three and a half metres. With the addition of the cylinder fitted on top, each complete unit is over 26 metres high and weighs 85 tonnes.

One for the personal archive…

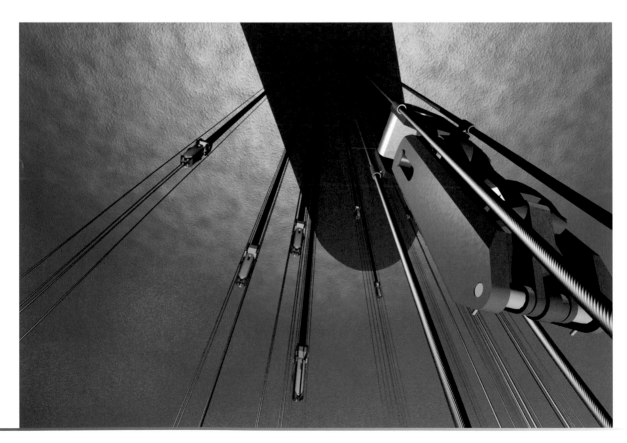

The first step is to lower four guide cables. These cables are fitted to a ring that is attached to a hole. The guide cables provide a direct line down which the grippers can be lowered. This method prevents the cables from turning and also ensures that the lifting cables don't get entangled. Each gripper plug has a unique shape that is a perfect fit. Once it has been fitted, the gripper opens and clamps itself to the underside of the sub's frame.

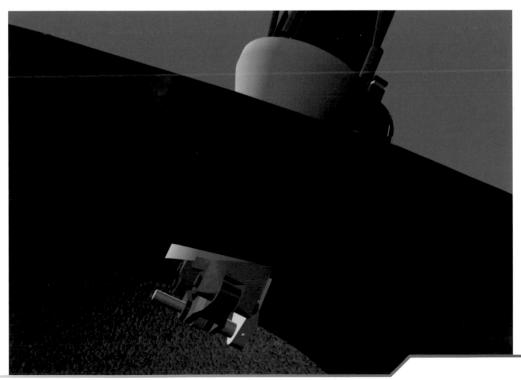

The lifting units are mounted on heave compensators, a type of shock absorber, to prevent sudden jolts to the lifting cables caused by the sea swells. This keeps the distance between the 'Kursk' and the lifting units constant at all times. The 'Giant 4' can now move up and down smoothly on the swells. The compensators can absorb a swell movement of up to three metres.

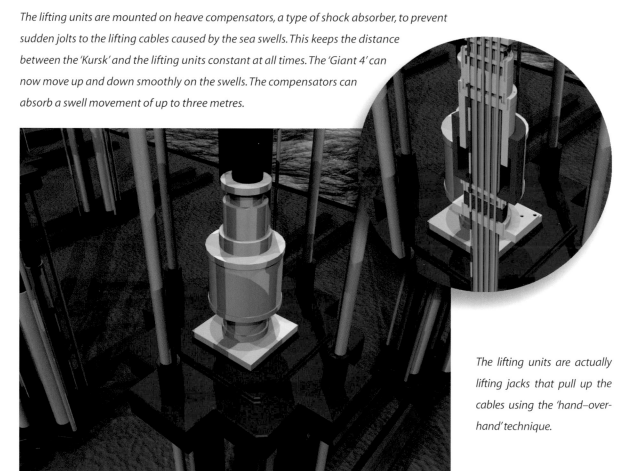

The lifting units are actually lifting jacks that pull up the cables using the 'hand–over–hand' technique.

As soon as the 'AMT Carrier' arrives and is positioned above the 'Kursk', the anchors are lowered to a depth of more than one hundred metres. The anchors and the sawing cable have to be positioned very precisely. As soon as this work has been completed, the sawing can begin.

In just a few hours, the first 33-metre long sawing cable fitted with 241 sleeves 'eats' its way through the first twenty per cent of the hull. Things are going well at this point but suddenly the cable snaps. The cable itself can easily be replaced, but a more serious problem is the snapping of the hoisting cable that runs along the suction anchors. This cable has been worn away on boulders lying close to the guiding wheel at the bottom of the suction anchor. There was no time to manufacture a protective cover for it but it is clear now that one will be needed. Divers fit steel plates to get around this problem but the job turns out to be easier said than done. For the first time, the salvors run into some delay.

All in all, five hoisting cables and four sawing cables break. Despite this, the net sawing time is 'just' 31 hours. This corresponds fairly closely to the theoretical sawing

Fifty-four steel cables are attached to each gripper.

An unsuspecting spectator…

SMIT

53

time of 24 hours calculated by the engineers. Rubin had thought the salvors were far too optimistic, as it had calculated that the sawing operation would take at least a week. Theo Haak is following the sawing operation from Rotterdam. He is kept informed daily by Paul Glerum and Arend van der Hoek, who are

Discussion on board the 'Mayo'.

supervising the work on the 'AMT Carrier'. On a couple of occasions, the sawing team is discouraged by setbacks, so Rotterdam has to work hard to keep their spirits up.

Anyway, they have to carry on, as there is no real alternative to sawing through the 'Kursk'. All the same, the loose items in the submarine that must not be removed and the possibility of unexploded torpedoes make this a task critical to the operation's success. However, the uncertainty regarding the

Photo taken from the 'Giant 4'. On the horizon, the Russian navy frigate 'Peter the Great'. The Russian navy stays in close proximity to the salvors throughout the operation.

state of the torpedoes disqualifies the only alternative, that of cutting the hull with water jets. Moreover, the latter method would take a lot of time: time that the salvors simply do not have.

Another factor is that the Russian President Putin has seized on the salvaging of the 'Kursk' as an opportunity to launch a media offensive, with glasnost (openness) winning out over secrecy. In the seaport of Murmansk, the Ice Palace has been converted into an international media centre. Dozens of Internet-enabled computers are set up to make it easy for the journalists to file their reports. The Russians are expecting more than a thousand journalists and TV and radio technicians. The centre is placed under the direct authority of Putin's assistant Sergei Yastrzembsky.

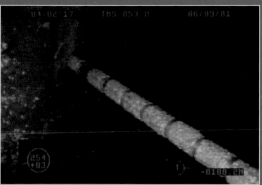

The wire in action on the 'Kursk'

Depiction of the cutting technique. The driving mechanism is mounted on top of the suction anchors located on either side of the 'Kursk'. During the cutting the anchors, which are actually hollow, drive themselves deeper into the seabed. This also draws the cable downward.

On board the 'Giant 4', last-minute modifications are being made to the equipment.

The diving bell on board the 'Mayo'. This diving bell lowers the divers (always three in number) to a depth of more than one hundred metres.

In the end, as expected, more than one thousand media centre passes are issued. A broad spectrum of the Russian media is represented and a twice-daily live bulletin is broadcast on all Russian TV stations. During the salvage operation, most of the Western correspondents in Russia are too busy reporting on the wake of the terrorist attacks in the United States and the expected attack on Afghanistan, which means that only a few dozen Western journalists remain in Murmansk. There is even a separate website where all information is made available in both Russian and English.

SMIT and Mammoet dispatch their spokespersons Lars Walder and Larissa van Seumeren to Murmansk to provide the journalists with all the information they need. It is a long time before the Russian media realises that sources other than the official ones may have important information too.

The sawing-off of the first compartment means that a very important stage has been reached, as the signal can now be given to start towing the 'Giant 4' to the Barents Sea. The ocean-going tug 'SmitWijs Singapore' tows the 'Giant 4' from the Norwegian port of Kirkenes to the 'Kursk's location. In the meantime, the divers work flat out to clean the 26 holes in the sub's hull. There is a huge jumble of cables and pipelines between the inner and outer hull. A sort of funnel has to be fitted above the holes to guide the grippers into the interior and to attach rings to which the guidelines, the 're-entry lines', will be attached. The purposes of these lines (four per gripper) is to prevent the grippers and lifting cables from 'spinning' and becoming entangled with one other. The funnels are needed because the 'Kursk' is not sitting flat on the seabed but is instead lying face down and at an angle in longitudinal and transverse directions. This means that the grippers have to be fitted at a certain angle.

The 52 people on board the 'Giant 4', captained by Piet Sinke from SMIT, are ready for action. Whilst in Kirkenes and en route, they have practised the entire operation countless times. The lifting units have been extensively tested and 'dry runs' have been carried out for all of the procedures, using the computer simulation programs.

Corporate Communications Managers Lars Walder (SMIT) and Larissa van Seumeren (Mammoet) inform the international media on a daily basis in a press center in Murmansk.

Piet Sinke looks after Mammoet's 'would-be sailors'. He instructs them in the basic principles of good seamanship. He also makes sure that everyone takes their boots off before entering the crew quarters, that the beds are changed when required, that the cabins are kept clean, that people shower and that everyone eats at the right time.

Jacob Hogendorp (left), SMIT's project leader for all the underwater work, discussing the progress of the salvage operation with a Russian admiral.

Just before the real lifting work begins, SMIT's Nico Buis (on the couch, left) and Mammoet's Frans van Seumeren (on the couch, right) arrive at Murmansk Airport. The two company chairmen are surrounded by a posse of journalists who want to know all there is to know about the salvage operation.

At the beginning of the final week of September, the lifting barge is in place over the 'Kursk'. Eight anchors and the same number of anchor cables, each of over seven hundred metres in length, anchor the 'Giant 4' in position. A looming depression luckily proves to be nothing more than a smudge on the weather chart. The ominous message is that at present the weather prospects are good but that more bad weather is 'lying in wait'. In fact, the 'Mayo' and the 'Giant 4' have already experienced their first brief snowstorms.

Right from the start, the salvors have said that their worst enemy will be the rapidly changing autumn weather conditions in the Barents Sea. The salvors are relying on detailed information from the Dutch Meteo Consult meteorological office. Weather forecasts are naturally also obtained from the Norwegian and Russian weather services and from the Russian navy's meteorological office. It turns out that the weather conditions are not only changeable but also unpredictable. This poses problems, as the salvors need three to five consecutive days of good weather in order to attach the 26 lifting cables to the 'Kursk' and lift it.

The heave compensation system ensures that dynamic forces arising in lifting wires due to the barge oscillations can be reduced to a safe level. Due to this system the barge can continue the lifting even during a storm. But the problem is that it is impossible to determine exactly a how the 'Giant 4' barge will behave. The eight anchors will be able to dampen down part of the barge's movements. A strong head-on wind would move the barge much less than a strong broadside wind would.

The 'Giant 4' is fully anchored down when a new depression delays the attaching of the lifting cables. It is not just bad weather but really severe weather. So severe, in fact, that the salvors even consider releasing the 'Giant 4' from its anchors and allowing it to seek shelter along the coast. The whole operation is now hanging by a thread. After all, it would take an extra day's work to re-position the barge. Moreover, another longish period of good weather would be required, and the chances of that get slimmer by the day. Captain Piet Sinke shoulders the responsibility and decides to leave his 'Giant 4' where it is.

Stormy weather on the Barents Sea. The weather has been generally well-disposed towards the salvors, but in early October a severe storm gets up.

The 'Mayo' and 'Giant 4' under bright lights. The operation proceeded round the clock, as time was of the essence.

Perhaps the prayers offered up by Priest Andrei from Murmansk proved effective. At the end of September, by order of the top naval officer, he was flown by helicopter to the cruiser 'Petr Velikiy', the flagship of the Northern Fleet from where the Russian Navy is coordinating the salvage operation. This first priest of the Svyato-Nikolsky cathedral in Murmansk has been given the facilities for a small chapel on board the cruiser. He is to remain on board until the end of the salvage operation.

For the people from Mammoet in particular, who are experiencing their first salvage operation on the open sea, the time spent on the Barents Sea is not always pleasant. 'Actually, it was an accumulation of disappointments', says Klaas Lamphen. 'On land, we don't give the weather and wind a wide berth. On land, you don't allow yourself to get blown off course so easily. At sea, things are different. This was something that we had no experience of.'

Despite this, most of the spare time is put to good use. There is much testing of the equipment to be used, and in addition many improvements to the equipment on board the 'Giant 4' are made to make it easier to operate during the actual lifting. Everything has to be secured again each time a storm is reported in the vicinity. The crew, not used to long periods of inactivity, throw themselves into a thrilling ludo competition.

After three days, the weather has brightened up again so much that a start can be made at attaching the lifting cables. The weather forecast is good too. On board the 'Giant 4' the crew have had a pretty hard time, mainly because conditions have not been good. The gentlemen sleep as well as dine in containers. One bright spot is that just before the storm broke a brief 'dry run' could be carried out regarding the lowering of the lifting cables and auxiliary cables to quickly attach the 26 grippers.

It is already October when the first lifting cable is attached to the 'Kursk'. The tension then just keeps increasing. A couple of good days of weather and…but no-one dares make any more predictions. The media centre in Murmansk gets busier and busier. The operation to attach the lifting cables proves difficult but, as all those involved tell each other, 'it's just a question of them getting a taste for it'.

On board the 'Giant 4', a temporary galley has been erected. Normally, the 'Giant 4' does not have any living quarters for crew, which is why several dozen containers have had to be sited on deck for the salvage workers to sleep and eat in. In an area just a couple of metres square, the cook prepares complete meals each day for 54 hungry salvage workers.

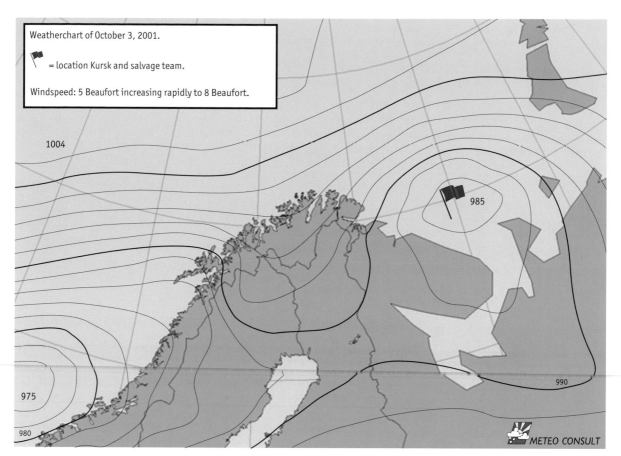

The weather chart for 3 October shows that there is a storm brewing. At all times, the weather forecasts play a key role in the success or failure of the operation. After all, the weather is the only element over which the salvors have no control. When the crew of the 'Giant 4' saw this chart, they stopped what they were doing and lashed down all the equipment.

Less than two days later It all goes wrong again. bad weather. And it docsn't hold back either. The forecast is that it won't just be the usual bad weather, but seriously bad weather. It is expected that no work will be possible for at least two days. And only six cables have been successfully attached. There is no longer any way back. The stay-behinds in Murmansk have never felt so low, but the mood on board both the salvage vessels 'Mayo' and 'Giant 4' is better than expected, as there they are still convinced that their mission will be a success. Jacob Hogendorp, on board the 'Mayo': 'Although things were very difficult from time to time, we all remained very positive. We knew that it could be done, but, well, the weather had to play ball.'

Just as unexpectedly as they appeared, the depressions disappear, or else turn out to be much less severe than forecast. This time, the storm puts in an appearance more than a day earlier than forecast. A positive point is that this time the weather prospects for the next few days are really positive. 'Now or never' is also the opinion of Jan Groot Bramel of the Meteo Consult meteorological office in Wageningen (NL), as his long-term forecast is for the expected seasonal weather and definitely not for the period of continuously good weather needed for this salvage job.

```
                                                  meteo consult bv
                                             agro business park 99-101
                                             p.o. box 617
                                             6700 ap wageningen
                                             the netherlands
                                             phone +31 (0) 317-399800
                                             fax +31 (0) 317-423164
                                             www.offshore.meteo.nl
```

```
To     : Kursk Salvage ( Mammoet and Smit International)
Attn   : Captain DSV Mayo
Email  : mayo_smitint@DSND.com, cvermeer@smitint.com, kjetil@havila.no
         leo.versluis@nl.mammoet.com
Subj.  : Special offshore weather forecast
Info.  : Duty forecaster at +31-(0)317-399800 or offshore@meteo.nl
Issued : Saturday,  6-OCT-2001 20:10 UTC
=================================================================

SYNOPSIS:
18 UTC - High pressure system (ridge) over Barents Sea is slowly drifting south. Ridge axis is
expected to cross Kursk location by 18 UTC tomorrow. Winds will back southwesterly and decrease
as a result. Meanwhile, northeasterly swell is expected to decrease gradually and become more
northerly. An occasional snow shower may still occur, but mainly dry conditions are expected.

GALE WARNINGS (next 24 hours):
none for next 24 hrs, risk of near gale on monday.

LOCATION: Barents_Sea                            POSITION:  69.4 N,  37.3 E
-----------------------------------------------------------------------------------
Time  | Wind/Gusts             | Wave height   Sea           Swell           | Vis.
utc   |    at 10m    at 50m    | sign./ max.   height per.   height    per.  |
      |    Kn        Kn        |  m  /  m       m   s         m         s    |
======|=====================|=============================================|========
Su 00 |  N 15/20     18/22     | 2.4 / 3.0     N 1.3  5      NNE 2.0   6    | good
Su 06 |  N 13/17     15/18     | 1.8 / 2.2     N 1.0  4      NNE 1.5   7    | good
Su 12 |  N  9/12     10/12     | 1.1 / 1.3     N 0.5  3      NNE 1.0   7    | good
Su 18 | WNW  7/ 9     8/10     | 1.0 / 1.0     WNW<0.5 3     NNE 1.0   7    | good
      |                        |                              |
Mo 00 | WSW  9-13/15 10-15/16  | 1.0 / 1.5     WSW 0.7  4     NNE 1.0   8    | good
Mo 12 | SSW 20-24/29 23-28/31  | 2.0 / 3.5     SSW 2.0  6     NNE 1.0   8    | mod
      | Rsk 25-29  Rsk 29-34   | Rsk  3.0                     |
      |                        |                              |
Tu 00 | WNW  5-11/13  6-13/13  | 1.0 / 1.5     WNW 0.5  3     SSE 1.0   7    | md/gd
Tu 12 |  NW  8-14/16  9-16/16  | 1.0 / 1.0      NW 0.5  4     ESE 0.7   7    | good
      |                        |                              |
We 00 | WNW  8-14/16  9-16/16  | 0.5 / 1.0     WNW 0.5  4     E   0.5   7    | good
We 12 |  W   4-10/12  5-11/12  | 0.5 / 1.0      W 0.5   3     WNW 0.5   5    | good
      |                        |                              |
Th 12 |  S   6-14/16  7-16/16  | 0.5 / 1.0      S 0.5   3     NNW 0.5   7    | md/gd
-----------------------------------------------------------------------------------

FURTHER OUTLOOK:
During Monday, a low pressure system will gain influence over the area with increasing southerly
winds. Its frontal system will also cross the area during that day, with snow at first,
gradually turning to sleet then rain. Visibility will become moderate or perhaps poor with risk
of fog later. Winds may back southeast for a time and by chance reach near gale force.
On Tuesday, the low's center is expected to cross the area with only light or moderate winds and
moderate easterly swell. Latest model output suggests winds should not increase significantly
afterwards.

Regards, Meteo Consult Holland
```

The weather forecast for Saturday 6 October, which shows a high pressure area approaching the location of the sunken 'Kursk'.
According to the forecast, the wind will drop, which will reduce the size of the swells. On the basis of this report, the team decides to
commence the lifting operation.

Suddenly, the operation to attach the lifting cables starts going smoothly. The day shift and the night shift start competing to see who can attach the greatest number of cables. Less than three days are needed to attach the remaining cables. The date is now Sunday 7 October. That evening, the first American bombs fall on Afghanistan. On board the 'Mayo', lifting coordinator Malcolm Dailey gives the signal that the lifting operation can begin.

Slowly but surely, the cables are drawn tight. This is the finale. Movement can already be discerned with the application of a so-called pre-stress of just one hundred and fifty tonnes or so on the 26 cables. This is a good sign, as it indicates that the dreaded 'stickiness' of the seabed is proving weaker than expected. The computers slowly increase the tension in the lifting cables. Greater force is exerted on the cables attached to the rear of the 'Kursk'. Once the sub's 'bottom' is pulled free, the rest will follow quickly, it is argued. The swell compensators (the shock

The 'Kursk' is pulled free of the seabed, after about 9,000 tonnes of pull force are applied to the cables. The sub is pulled up tight under the 'Giant 4' at a speed of 10 metres per hour, a task that takes a little over 10 hours.

absorbers) work extremely well. On the deck, all 26 lifting units move up and down individually. It's a strange sight to see such enormous pieces of equipment moving in this way.

That Sunday evening, Frans van Seumeren and Nico Buis join those on board the 'Mayo'. They have flown in by helicopter from Murmansk to give the crews that extra bit of encouragement, but severe snowstorms mean their return flight has to be grounded. Rubin boss Igor Spassky and vice admiral Barskov have been on the 'Mayo' for a week already. Now they sit there with Nico Buis and Frans van Seumeren in front of all of the monitors, like schoolboys. The tension rises even higher.

Meanwhile in Rotterdam, at the SMIT head office, the crisis team is set up. Project leaders and senior management of both companies are in close contact with the salvage team at the scene. During the entire night they follow the operation. Nobody allows themselves to some sleep.

The problem is that no-one knows how much the 'Kursk' actually weighs in its present condition. Has the sub completely filled up with water or does it still contain a lot of air? And how will the vessel's centre of gravity behave if the rear is lifted first or if the body of water in the 'Kursk' starts sliding? It is not just a question of freeing the 'Kursk' but also of keeping it under control once it has been freed.

According to Rubin, the 'Kursk's maximum weight is 9,500 tonnes and the minimum 8,300 tonnes. The suction force from the seabed proves to be much less than expected. After just four hours of pulling, the 'Kursk' comes free. Just 9,000 tonnes of pull force have been required. During the lifting operation, the sub's weight is recorded as 8,860 tonnes. On Monday morning 8 October, at a quarter to four local time (a quarter to two in The Netherlands), the 'Kursk' is in a state of suspension, six metres above the seabed and safe in the arms of the 'Giant 4's hoists.

The actual lift. Air bubbles prove that the "Kursk" is moving!

On board the 'Mayo', everyone hugs each other. Rubin boss Spassky and the two directors can hardly contain their emotions and find it difficult to hold back the tears. The most important phase of the entire salvage operation has been a success, and it is worth remembering that many people have worked around the clock for months to get to this point.

The satisfaction is evident on their faces, as the lifting system has worked perfectly.

The 'SmitWijs Singapore' seen from the 'Giant 4', en route to Murmansk.

THE JOURNEY HOME

During the last preparation for the 'Kursk' lifting they start to unmoor the 'Giant 4'. Now when the 'Kursk' has been freed from the floor of the Barents Sea and lifted by 10 meters, Captain Piet Sinke gives the signal that the 'Giant 4' can be uncoupled from its anchors completely. At a speed of ten metres per hour, the 'Kursk' is raised until it is held tight under the lifting barge. While the lifting is still in progress, the barge's course is being set for Murmansk, towed by the tug 'SmitWijs Singapore'. However, the situation is still tense, as the question is whether the sub's conning towers will actually fit into the opening cut for them in the underside of the 'Giant 4' and also whether the 'saddles' fitted under the lifting barge will fit properly. None of these things have been tested before.

The 'Giant 4-Kursk' 'combination' is towed to the port of Murmansk by the ocean-going tug 'SmitWijs Singapore'.

The main problem here is the last little bit, i.e. once the 'Kursk', rocking in its hoists, has been hoisted to hang a metre under the heaving 'Giant 4', how should this last little bit of lifting be tackled: with the help of the strandjacks or by using the sea swell compensation system? At that particular moment the weather is calm, so the jacks are used to pull the 'Kursk' tight up against the underside of the 'Giant 4'.

This is an enormous relief for all those concerned. However, there is no time to celebrate the success of the lifting operation, although Piet Sinke has asked cook Ruud de Keijzer to bake a big cake that is decorated with the date and time of the hoisting up of the 'Kursk', piped on in whipped cream. The Russian navy places a floral wreath on the water above the site of the 'Kursk's grave and a school of dolphins appears from nowhere. The Russians see this as a salute to the crew who perished in the sub and to the salvage crews.

Once in Murmansk, the bad weather starts in earnest. It is now mid-October and winter is approaching fast. The deck of the 'Giant 4' is quickly covered by a snow-white blanket.

The lifting of the 'Kursk' is followed by the final (and important) phase, namely its towing to a dock. The 'Giant 4' with the 'Kursk' under it is too deep in the water to enter the dock, so the whole combination has to be lifted. Two huge semi-submersible barges are constructed for this purpose and have to raise the combined 'Giant 4' with the 'Kursk' underneath, so that they can be towed into dock.

The combination of the 'Giant 4' and 'Kursk' lies in the middle of the bay at Murmansk, as the barges are brought alongside. The barges are then sunk by allowing them to fill with water. When they have sunk sufficiently far, they are pulled under the 'Giant 4' and secured to it. Next, the water is pumped out of the barges, which rise slowly.

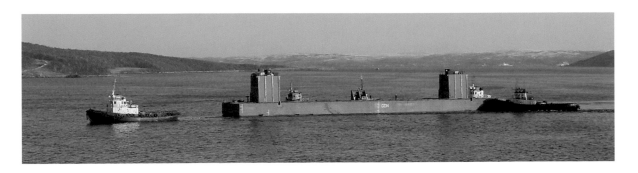

A sub barge is manoeuvred into place alongside the 'Giant 4', where it will be sunk. Once under water, the barge will be pushed under the 'Giant 4' and the water will be pumped out again.

Panorama of the dock in the bay at Murmansk.

The Russian media report extensively on the successful operation. Vice-premier Ilya Klebanov who has been stayin onboard the cruiser 'Petr Velikiy' during the lifting operation, publicly praises the salvors, saying that they have carried out their job 'professionally and with a sense of responsibility.' Congratulations from all over the world pour into the headquarters of both SMIT and Mammoet .

However, the raising of the 'Kursk' from the seabed does not mean that the salvage operation has been completed, as the 'Kursk' still has to be transported to a huge dock at the Russian village Roslyakov. The route they will take to get there is not entirely without risk either, and there is still an important job to be carried out before the 'Kursk' can be brought into dock. This is because the combination of the 'Giant 4' and 'Kursk' lies too deep in the water to enter the sunken dock, so they are to be hoisted up together using two auxiliary barges specially built for this purpose.

The route to Belokamennaya Bay in the fjord near Murmansk is completed without any problems. The bay lies directly opposite the Roslyakovo naval base. There, the two auxiliary barges are to be positioned halfway under the 'Giant 4'.

By the time that the water has been pumped out of the barges, the 'Giant 4' and 'Kursk' have been raised more than six metres in the water.

The whole floating hulk is now so high in the water that it can be manoeuvred into the dock, where the 'Kursk' is carefully positioned on supports.

Upon their arrival in the bay on 10 October, the salvors are greeted by loud hooting and honking from dozens of ships' hooters. On the shore stand dozens of people, including surviving relatives of the crew that perished in the 'Kursk'. Russian navy divers immediately start inspecting the sub. They also discover that sections of the sub's forward part will still have to be sawn off before the 'Kursk' can be brought into the dock.

For half the salvage team, their task is now over and they can go home, whilst the other half must stay behind for the final, although not the least important, part of the operation. The two auxiliary barges 'Mar' and 'Gon' have to lift the 'Giant 4' several metres out of the water, a total weight of 22,000 tonnes.

The winter weather in Northern Russia has now taken a turn for the (much) worse. The temporary accommodation on board the 'Giant 4' was not built for these low temperatures and it is not long before the water pipes freeze up. This problem is overcome with the help of a burner. Life jackets are cut into pieces and pressed into service as insulating material. Tiredness takes its toll and a vicious flu virus spreads like wildfire - almost no one escapes its attention.

The 'Mar' and 'Gon' are not as stable as people would like. In fact, the 'Mar', which is the first to be submerged and positioned halfway under the 'Giant 4', is almost lost.
At dawn on Sunday 21 October, the 'Kursk', together with the 'Giant 4' borne by the two auxiliary barges, begins the final section of its 'journey home' to the dock.

At SMIT, they have bad memories of this huge, 300-metre long, 88-metre wide and 30-metre high dock that the 'Kursk' has to be delivered to. In the autumn of 1979, the tugs 'Smit Londen' and 'Smit Rotterdam' towed the then brand-new dock from the shipyard close to the Swedish town of Gothenburg to the Arctic Cape and further east to Murmansk. Just after passing the Arctic Cape, the tugs and cargo hit a bad weather front and decided to seek refuge in the fjord near Kirkenes, Norway.

That was when the blustery wind picked up even more; at storm force 10 the fjord was able to offer precious little protection. The dock, which has a lateral surface of nine thousand square metres, acted like a huge wind catcher. 'Smit Rotterdam' and 'Smit Londen' were unable to hold onto their cargo because the cables snapped in the violent autumn storm. The dock started drifting and an attempt to anchor it to the rocks failed. In the end, the dock actually hit the rocks.

SMIT had no option but to salvage the dock and tow it back to the Swedish shipyard. Close on a year later, it was towed to Murmansk again. This time there were no problems. More than twenty years later, SMIT is 'reunited' with the dock.

Snowgusts, arctic temperatures and a strong headwind make the crossing from the fjord to the dock difficult. This part of the operation is being managed by the Russian navy, and fifty seamen have already been dropped onto the 'Giant 4' to help moor the combination of the 'Giant 4' and 'Kursk' in the dock.

The combined 'Giant 4-Kursk' hulk is slowly towed into the dock.

Once on the other side of the fjord, it turns out that the combination of the 'Giant 4' and 'Kursk' and auxiliary barges is still too low in the water. Two hundred tonnes of equipment are quickly hoisted off the deck of the 'Giant 4' and 400 tonnes of ballast water are pumped overboard.

The Russians make great efforts. The navy plays it safe and deploys no fewer than ten tugs for the journey into dock. In addition to the tugs, there are small boats that have been given the role of positioning the 'Kursk' precisely above the dock's blocks. Everyone wants to help bring the lost comrades into port.

Once the 'Kursk' has been positioned precisely above the dock blocks, more pandemonium ensues. By means of a complex interplay of people and equipment, in which a number of interpreters play a leading role, the dock is slowly raised while the jacks on the 'Giant 4' carefully lower the 'Kursk'. The next morning, the salvors see the 'Kursk' for the first time and carefully walk along the top of the sub to remove the grippers.

The next day, the 'Giant 4', this time without the 'Kursk', floats out of the dock on the two auxiliary barges. Piet Sinke feels that the salvage crews shouldn't leave without a proper farewell and has ordered a special wreath for the occasion. As soon as they have left the dock, all the remaining salvors gather on the quarter-deck of the 'Giant 4' while Sinke makes a brief speech. Sinke: 'Then it was caps off and mouths shut for a minute's silence. The Russians very much appreciated this gesture. We felt that it was the least we could do.'

The 'Mar' and the 'Gon' are disconnected without any problem. Barely a week later the 'Giant 4', towed by the 'SmitWijs Singapore', arrives in the Norwegian port of Kirkenes. A fresh crew is to pilot the 'Giant 4' home. Within two hours of arriving, Captain Piet Sinke and the last remaining salvors are on a plane flying back to The Netherlands.

As soon as the salvors have delivered the 'Kursk' to the dock, the Russian Prosecutor-General Vladimir Ustinov and his team start the investigation into the circumstances surrounding the sinking of the 'Kursk'. Ustinov has put together eight teams of specialists to carry out at least twenty separate investigations and other work, including the task of removing the remains of the crew. Another job is the careful removal of the cruise missiles from the wreck.

According to the head of the investigation Ustinov, it has been established that at the time of the accident no other vessel was in the neighbourhood of the 'Kursk'. The submarine was sunk by an explosion in a torpedo to be used for the exercises. The cause of the explosion was not made public. Admiral Kuroyedov adds that the fuel in the torpedo, hydrogen peroxide, is extremely unstable. Western navies banned the use of this fuel for torpedoes after an accident on board the British sub HMS Sidon in 1955.

The job has been more or less completed, and people can smile with relief again.
Captain Piet Sinke completes his paperwork, assisted by a Russian servicewoman.

Prosecutor-General Ustinov also reveals that the final hours of the crew on board the 'Kursk' must have been hell. Most of the crew and passengers were killed almost immediately by the two powerful explosions, whilst those that survived succumbed to carbon monoxide poisoning in the hours that followed.

At the end of November 2001, the Dutch salvage crews are welcomed to the Kremlin by President Putin with all honours. President Putin takes this opportunity to describe the salvage operation as 'a unique example of international cooperation'. In their own country, the Dutch Minister of Transport and Public Works Netelenbos honours the salvors by awarding them the Michiel de Ruyter medal.

During the reception in the Kremlin, Russian President Putin also reveals how difficult the whole lifting operation was and that the decision to carry out the operation was not an easy one for him personally. The Russian Government and Naval Command were against the submarine lifting. Recollecting the day of 19 August 2000, the day when he made the decision to lift the 'Kursk', Putin says that only one person firmly stated that the lifting was possible and required. That is why the President later on entrusted just him with the responsibility for arrangement for the lifting operation. And the result proves the correctness and validity of the taken decision.

Once in the dock, the water level is lowered and the 'Kursk' is raised above the waterline. Salvage workers stand on the deck of the submarine ready to untie it and position it on the supports. The entire length of the conning tower of the 'Kursk' can be seen at bottom.

The 'Kursk' has come home too. The conning tower ▶ of the 'Kursk' rises above the waterline. For the salvage workers, this means that all their work is now done. The Russians commence the task of identifying the bodies and dismantling the two reactors.

The salvage workers' task is complete, and the 'Giant 4' can leave the dock again. Before it sets sail, a closing ceremony is held in memoriam of the lost crewmembers of the 'Kursk'. A wreath is placed in the water and Captain Piet Sinke asks for a minute's silence.

Russian marines on the deck of the 'Giant 4'.
They walk round, amazed at the size of the
vessel that brought back their lost comrades.

The salvage team on board of the 'Giant 4'.

The homecoming. At Amsterdam's Schiphol Airport, the salvors are welcomed by dozens of their relatives waving banners and flowers. The press is there too and reports on all aspects of the homecoming.

s je bent een Giant 4 us !

The offices of SMIT and Mammoet are inundated with congratulatory messages. The lobby of the SMIT offices is bedecked with hundreds of letters, cards and faxes congratulating the salvage workers on their hard work and impressive achievement.

The bay at Murmansk.

TECHNICAL DRAWINGS

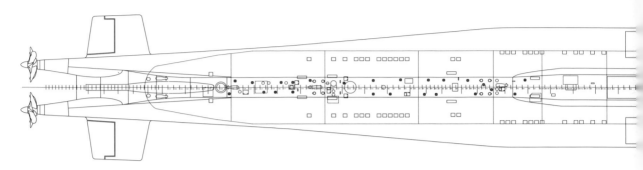

TOP VIEW

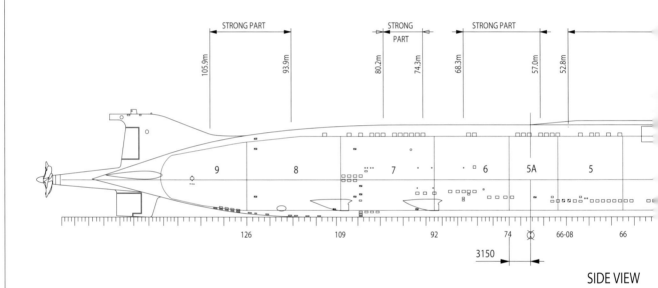

SIDE VIEW

Cross-section of the 'Kursk'. The foremost compartment that housed the torpedoes was completely destroyed in the explosion. The reactors were located in compartment 6.

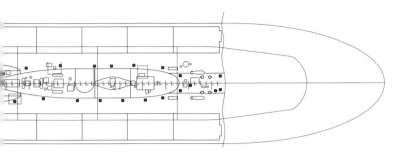

STRONG PART

0m

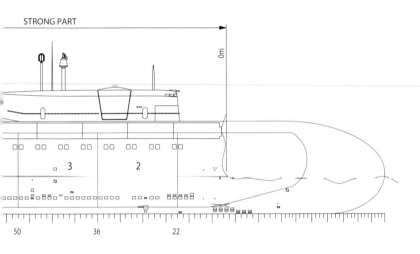

3   2

50   36   22

CROSS SECTION

Remarks:

Drawing represents Kursk in damaged condition.
On bottom weight: 9200 ton.

Main particulars:

Length o.a.   : 154m (design)
Length o.a.   : 130m (damaged)
Width o.a.   : 18.2m
Depth   : 13.7m (excl. sail)
Depth   : 18.3m (incl. sail & masts)
Draught   : 9.5m (surfaced)
Pressure hull   : 11m (diameter)

Rev	Date	Drawn	Description	Chkd	E.Appr	P.Appr	Client	Date
C4	13-Dec-00	GVe	FOR USE, UPDATED	HvH	CLa	BKa		
C3	21-Nov-00	GVe	FOR USE, UPDATED	HvH	HHo	BKa		
C2	17-Oct-00	GVe	FOR USE, UPDATED	HvH	HHo	BKa		
C1	21-Sep-00	PSI	FOR USE, UPDATED	GVe	HHo	BKa		
C	11-Sep-00	PSI	FOR USE	GVe	HHo	BKa		
A	11-Sep-00	PSI	FOR INTERNAL REVIEW	GVe	HHo	BKa		

Subject

GENERAL ARRANGEMENT KURSK

Project

RECOVERY "KURSK"

Client

RUBIN

SMIT Engineering

P.O.Box 1042, 3000 BA Rotterdam

CAD-drwg not to be changed manually

Orig. Size   A3

Scale	Drawing No	Sheet	Rev
1:500	00.12.040-D-001	1 of 1	C4

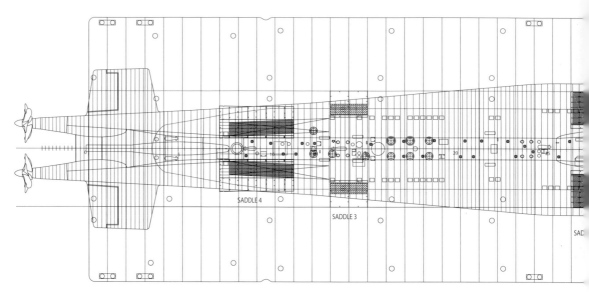

TOP VIEW

Depiction of the 'Giant 4', with underneath it the 'Kursk'. The large black areas show the points where the saddles were attached. These saddles have the same shape as the 'Kursk'. Once the sub has been pulled up under the 'Giant 4', the saddles 'clamp' it even more tightly under the salvage vessel.

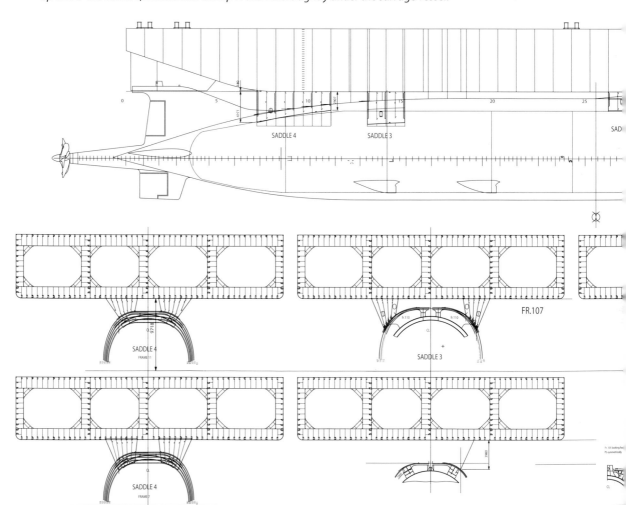

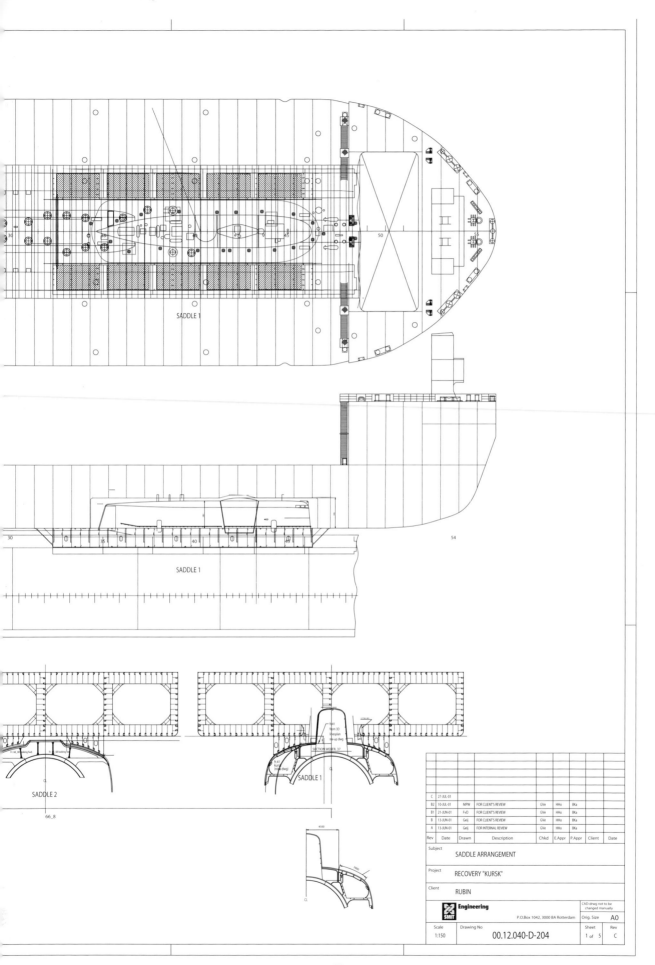

SADDLE 1

SADDLE 1

SADDLE 2

SADDLE 1

C	27-JUL-01						
B2	10-JUL-01	MPW	FOR CLIENT'S REVIEW	GVe	HHo	BKa	
B1	21-JUN-01	FvD	FOR CLIENT'S REVIEW	GVe	HHo	BKa	
B	13-JUN-01	Geij	FOR CLIENT'S REVIEW	GVe	HHo	BKa	
A	13-JUN-01	Geij	FOR INTERNAL REVIEW	GVe	HHo	BKa	
Rev	Date	Drawn	Description	Chkd	E.Appr	P.Appr	Client	Date

Subject
SADDLE ARRANGEMENT

Project
RECOVERY "KURSK"

Client
RUBIN

SMIT Engineering

P.O.Box 1042, 3000 BA Rotterdam

CAD-drwg not to be changed manually

Orig. Size: A0

Scale	Drawing No		Sheet	Rev
1:150	00.12.040-D-204		1 of 5	C

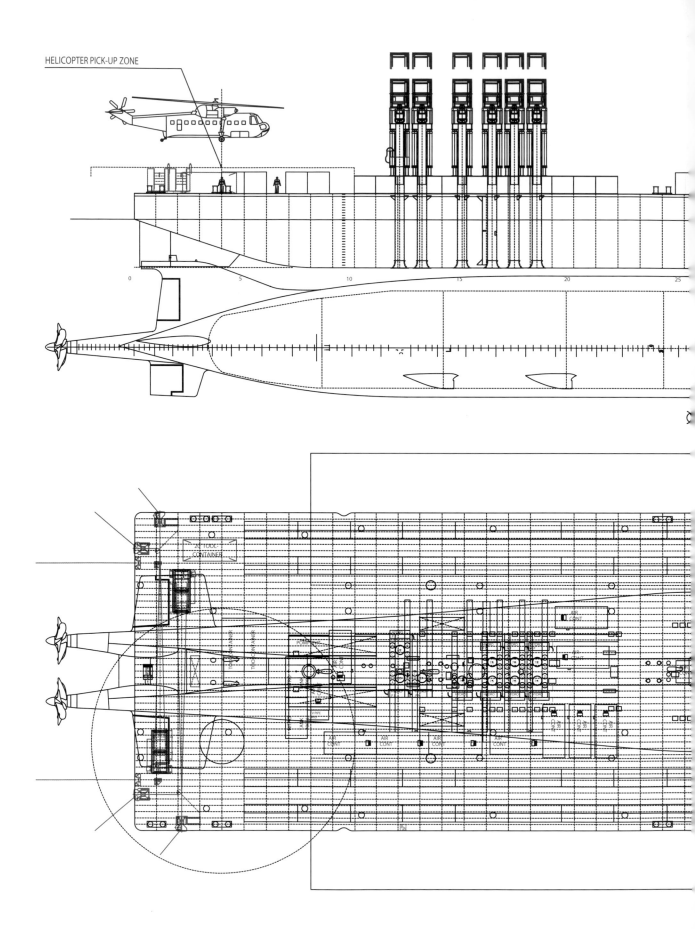

HELICOPTER PICK-UP ZONE

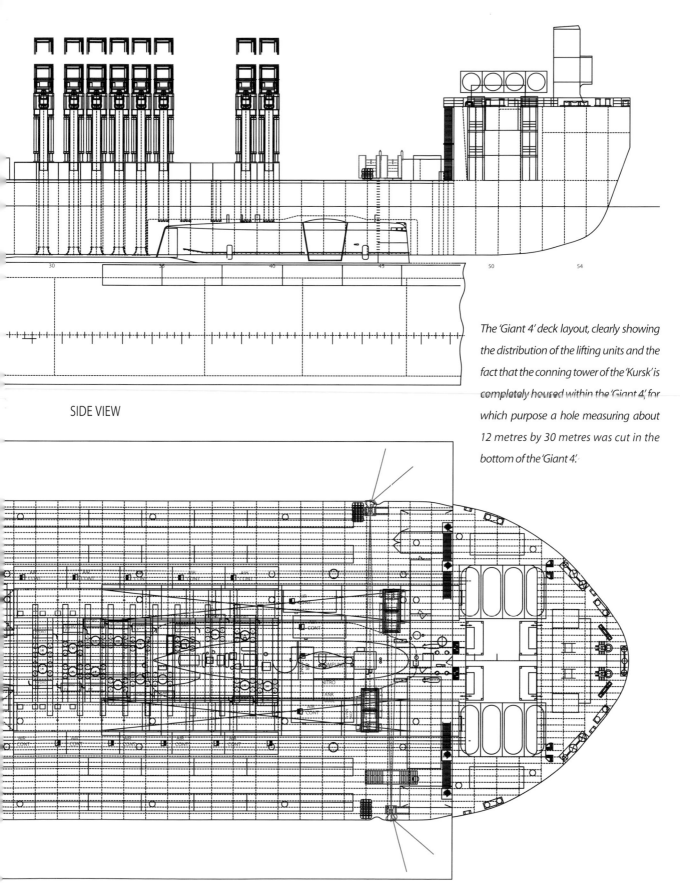

SIDE VIEW

The 'Giant 4' deck layout, clearly showing the distribution of the lifting units and the fact that the conning tower of the 'Kursk' is completely housed within the 'Giant 4', for which purpose a hole measuring about 12 metres by 30 metres was cut in the bottom of the 'Giant 4'.

DECK LAYOUT - TOP VIEW

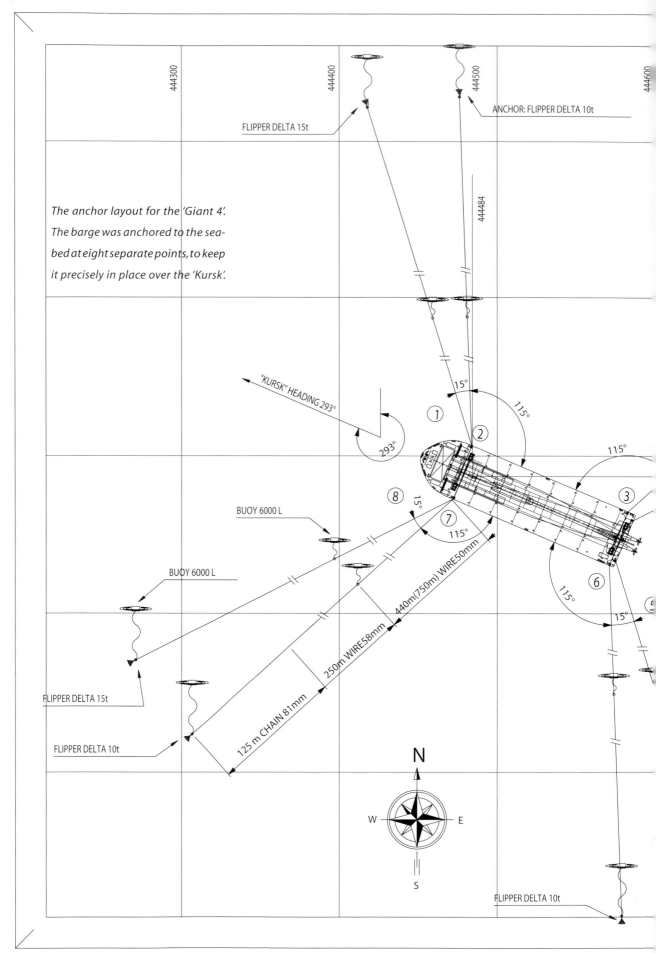

The anchor layout for the 'Giant 4'. The barge was anchored to the seabed at eight separate points, to keep it precisely in place over the 'Kursk'.

FLIPPER DELTA 15t

ANCHOR: FLIPPER DELTA 10t

444300

444400

444500

444600

444484

"KURSK" HEADING 293°

293°

15°

115°

115°

15°

① ② ③

⑧ ⑦ ⑥ ⑤

15° 115°

115°

BUOY 6000 L

BUOY 6000 L

440m(750m) WIRE 50mm

250m WIRE 58mm

125 m CHAIN 81mm

FLIPPER DELTA 15t

FLIPPER DELTA 10t

FLIPPER DELTA 10t

N
W E
S

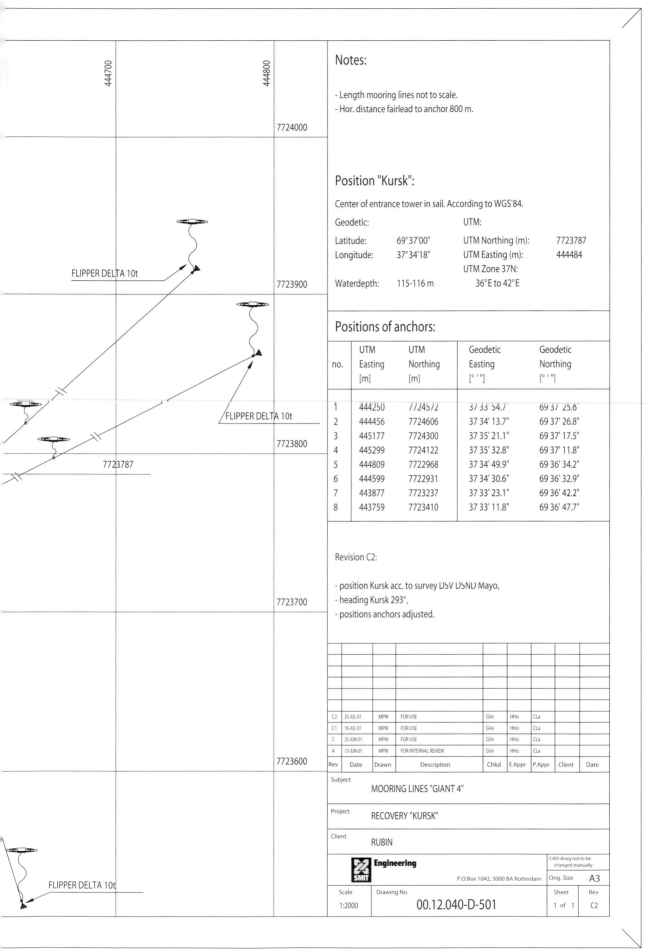

Notes:

- Length mooring lines not to scale.
- Hor. distance fairlead to anchor 800 m.

Position "Kursk":

Center of entrance tower in sail. According to WGS'84.

Geodetic:		UTM:	
Latitude:	69°37'00"	UTM Northing (m):	7723787
Longitude:	37°34'18"	UTM Easting (m):	444484
		UTM Zone 37N:	
Waterdepth:	115-116 m	36°E to 42°E	

Positions of anchors:

no.	UTM Easting [m]	UTM Northing [m]	Geodetic Easting [° ' "]	Geodetic Northing [° ' "]
1	444250	7724572	37 33' 54.7"	69 37' 25.8"
2	444456	7724606	37 34' 13.7"	69 37' 26.8"
3	445177	7724300	37 35' 21.1"	69 37' 17.5"
4	445299	7724122	37 35' 32.8"	69 37' 11.8"
5	444809	7722968	37 34' 49.9"	69 36' 34.2"
6	444599	7722931	37 34' 30.6"	69 36' 32.9"
7	443877	7723237	37 33' 23.1"	69 36' 42.2"
8	443759	7723410	37 33' 11.8"	69 36' 47.7"

Revision C2:

- position Kursk acc. to survey DSV DSND Mayo,
- heading Kursk 293°,
- positions anchors adjusted.

Rev	Date	Drawn	Description	Chkd	E.Appr	P.Appr	Client	Date
C2	25-JUL-01	MPW	FOR USE	GVe	HHo	CLa		
C1	16-JUL-01	MPW	FOR USE	GVe	HHo	CLa		
C	25-JUN-01	MPW	FOR USE	GVe	HHo	CLa		
A	13-JUN-01	MPW	FOR INTERNAL REVIEW	GVe	HHo	CLa		

Subject	MOORING LINES "GIANT 4"
Project	RECOVERY "KURSK"
Client	RUBIN

Engineering SMIT

P.O.Box 1042, 3000 BA Rotterdam

CAD-drwg not to be changed manually

Orig. Size: A3

Scale	Drawing No	Sheet	Rev
1:2000	00.12.040-D-501	1 of 1	C2

FLIPPER DELTA 10t

FLIPPER DELTA 10t

FLIPPER DELTA 10t

7724000
7723900
7723800
7723787
7723700
7723600

444700
444800

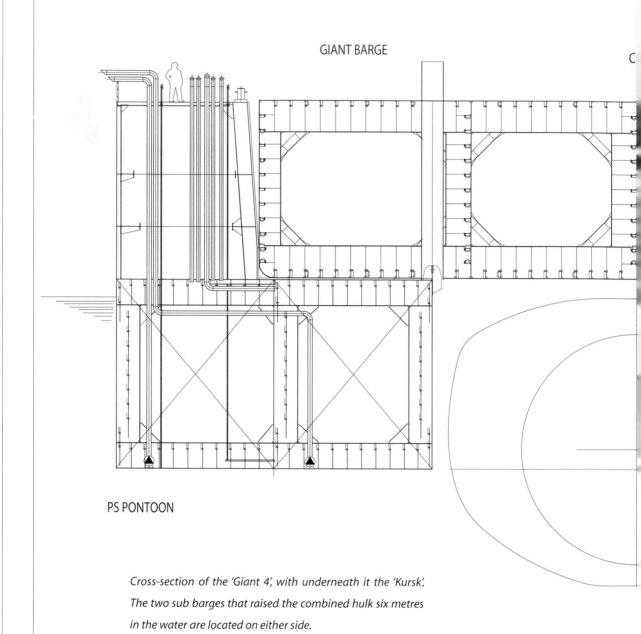

GIANT BARGE

C

PS PONTOON

Cross-section of the 'Giant 4', with underneath it the 'Kursk'.
The two sub barges that raised the combined hulk six metres
in the water are located on either side.

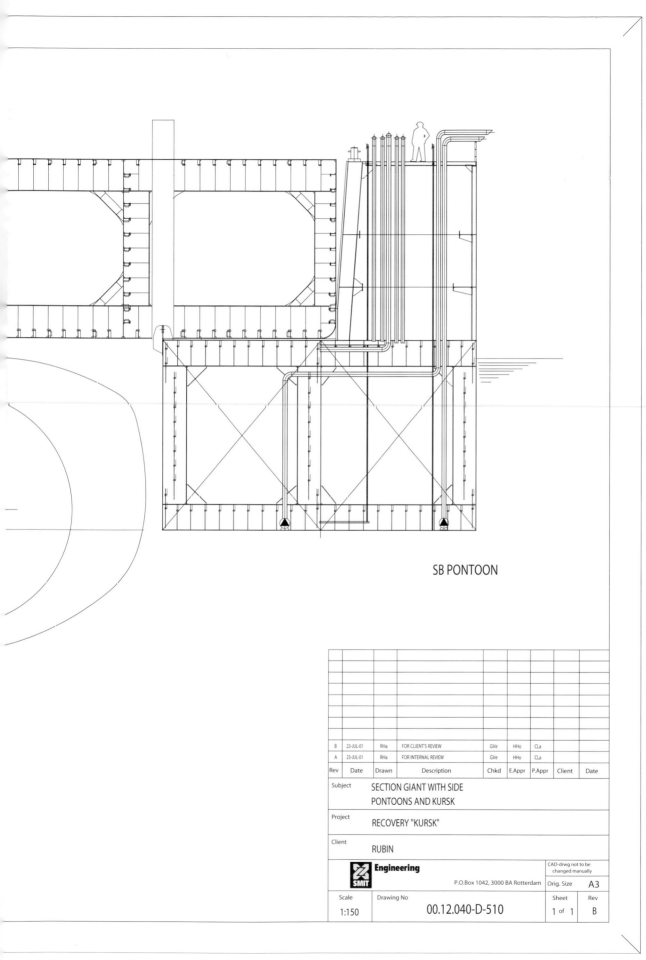

SB PONTOON

B	23-JUL-01	RHa	FOR CLIENT'S REVIEW	GVe	HHo	CLa		
A	23-JUL-01	RHa	FOR INTERNAL REVIEW	GVe	HHo	CLa		
Rev	Date	Drawn	Description	Chkd	E.Appr	P.Appr	Client	Date

Subject	SECTION GIANT WITH SIDE PONTOONS AND KURSK
Project	RECOVERY "KURSK"
Client	RUBIN

SMIT Engineering	CAD-drwg not to be changed manually
P.O.Box 1042, 3000 BA Rotterdam	Orig. Size A3

Scale	Drawing No	Sheet	Rev
1:150	00.12.040-D-510	1 of 1	B

COMPANY PROFILE

SMIT has a proud tradition of more than 160 years of service in the maritime sector. The company has earned an excellent reputation by combining expertise and experience with high-quality materials and equipment. SMIT aims to provide its services in the main to shipping companies, producers in the oil and LNG industries, insurers and governments. SMIT maintains the highest standards in respect of Safety, Health, the protection of the Environment and Quality.

SMIT's services are organised into four Divisions:

- **Harbour Towage**: harbour towage services and related maritime services.
- **Terminals**: towage services and related maritime and management services to offshore and onshore terminals.
- **Salvage**: salvage, wreck removal, environmental protection and consultancy.
- **Transport & Heavy Lift**: barge rental & transport, ocean, coastal and river towage, heavy lifting and marine support to a variety of civil and offshore projects.

SMIT's strategy is orientated towards strengthening the above activities and in building on its leading position in these sectors.

The company aims to achieve sustained improvement in its profitability, through autonomous growth and selective acquisitions in the Harbour Towage and Terminals Divisions, as well as through cost control and effective economies of scale across all Divisions.

The company operates according to principles that recognise its responsibilities towards its clients, employees, shareholders and partners, and to society in general. SMIT has incorporated its objectives into the following 'Vision' and 'Mission':

SMIT'S VISION

To be the leading player in the global market for maritime services,

preferred by customers due to the high perceived added value of its integrated package of service offerings.

- **Leading player**: to be first or second in all selected businesses.
- **Global market**: to operate on a worldwide scale.
- **Maritime services**: to be active in professional services on/around water.
- **Integrated package**: to offer customers a family of services tailored to their needs.
- **High perceived added value**: to focus on highly regarded specialist services.

SMIT'S MISSION

SMIT is a maritime service provider, with the world's seas and harbours as its field of operation.

We value the combination of expertise, inventiveness and specialized equipment as the key ingredients towards offering our customers the high quality solutions they require. We strive to fulfil the needs of five critical stakeholder groups:

- **Customers**: to deliver a high quality service tailored to customers' specific needs.
- **Employees**: to offer challenging work, personal development opportunities and a clear career perspective.
- **Shareholders**: to offer corporate transparency and to create shareholder value.
- **Partners**: to cooperate on the basis of mutual respect and mutual benefit.
- **Society**: to act with due care for the environment and the community.

The following companies contributed to the success of the salvage of the 'Kursk':

Aggreko Nederland B.V.	The Netherlands	Ingenieursgemeinschaft IgH	Germany
Albers Ingenieursbureau	The Netherlands	Kimek	Norway
Anchor Marine Transport Ltd.	United Kingdom	Kirkenes Shipping A.S.	Norway
Antwerp Safety Centre	Belgium	Large and Associates	United Kingdom
Bezemer Dordrecht B.V.	The Netherlands	LGH Verhuur Hijsmateriaal B.V.	The Netherlands
Boekestijn Kraanverhuur	The Netherlands	Majestic Products B.V.	The Netherlands
Briggs Marine Contractors Ltd.	United Kingdom	Marinco Survey B.V.	The Netherlands
Bureau Verweij	The Netherlands	Maritiem Trainingscentrum B.V.	The Netherlands
Catering Logistics Management	The Netherlands	Meteo Consult	The Netherlands
Copipe Sytems Ltd.	United Kingdom	NCA A.S.	Norway
De Haas Maassluis B.V.	The Netherlands	Pommec Diving Equipment	The Netherlands
Decam	The Netherlands	Rexroth Hydrocare B.V.	The Netherlands
Dirkzwager Royal Agencies	The Netherlands	Rulewave B.V.	The Netherlands
DSND Subsea Ltd.	United Kingdom	Safety Service Center	The Netherlands
Duffy & McGovern Acc. Serv.	United Kingdom	Scheepssloperij Nederland B.V.	The Netherlands
Econosto	The Netherlands	Schiepo Services B.V.	The Netherlands
Elektricom	The Netherlands	Sea Salvage S.L.	Spain
Emergency Medical Care	The Netherlands	Seatools B.V.	The Netherlands
Euro Offshore B.V.	The Netherlands	Shipdock Amsterdam B.V.	The Netherlands
Fischcon Trading & Engineering BV	The Netherlands	Skadoc Submersible Vehicles	The Netherlands
Frank Mohn Flatoy A.S.	Norway	Sledge Hammer Engineering Int. B.V.	The Netherlands
Grofsmederij Nieuwkoop B.V.	The Netherlands	Submersible Television Survey	United Kingdom
GSHydro Benelux B.V.	The Netherlands	Suction Pile Technology	The Netherlands
GTI Marine & Offshore	The Netherlands	Tenwolde Transport & Repairs	The Netherlands
Hapo International Barges B.V.	The Netherlands	Thofex B.V. Handelsonderneming	The Netherlands
Havilla Supply Ships Ltd.	Norway	TNO Industries	The Netherlands
Hebu Techniek B.V.	The Netherlands	Touw Expertise en Ingenieursbureau	The Netherlands
Holland Offshore Consulting	The Netherlands	TQ3 Travel Solutions	The Netherlands
Holland Special Pumps B.V.	The Netherlands	Vlaardingen Oost Scheepsreparaties	The Netherlands
Holmatro Ind. & Resc. Equipment	The Netherlands	Vlierodam Handelsmij.	The Netherlands
HPC Holland Perslucht B.V.	The Netherlands	Vopak Agencies B.V.	The Netherlands
Huisman-Itrec	The Netherlands	Wakker Zeilmakerij	The Netherlands
Hydac B.V.	The Netherlands	Widia Nederland B.V.	The Netherlands
Hydrasun	The Netherlands	World Marine Support B.V.	The Netherlands
Hydroplus B.V.	The Netherlands	Zwatra B.V.	The Netherlands
Hydrospex Cylap B.V.	The Netherlands		

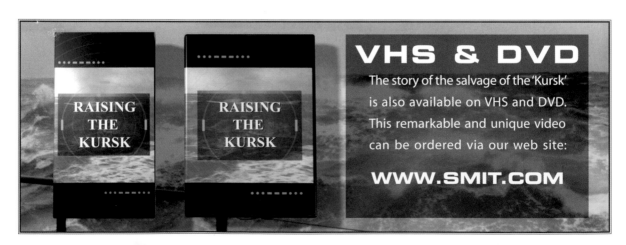